RHCSA EXAM PASS

RED HAT CERTIFIED SYSTEM ADMINISTRATOR STUDY GUIDE

4 BOOKS IN 1

BOOK 1
RHCSA EXAM PASS: FOUNDATIONS OF LINUX ADMINISTRATION

BOOK 2
RHCSA EXAM PASS: ADVANCED SYSTEM CONFIGURATION AND MANAGEMENT

BOOK 3
RHCSA EXAM PASS: NETWORK ADMINISTRATION AND SECURITY

BOOK 4
RHCSA EXAM PASS: PERFORMANCE TUNING AND TROUBLESHOOTING TECHNIQUES

ROB BOTWRIGHT

Published by Rob Botwright
Library of Congress Cataloging-in-Publication Data
ISBN 978-1-83938-776-0
Cover design by Rizzo

Disclaimer

The contents of this book are based on extensive research and the best available historical sources. However, the author and publisher make no claims, promises, or guarantees about the accuracy, completeness, or adequacy of the information contained herein. The information in this book is provided on an "as is" basis, and the author and publisher disclaim any and all liability for any errors, omissions, or inaccuracies in the information or for any actions taken in reliance on such information. The opinions and views expressed in this book are those of the author and do not necessarily reflect the official policy or position of any organization or individual mentioned in this book. Any reference to specific people, places, or events is intended only to provide historical context and is not intended to defame or malign any group, individual, or entity. The information in this book is intended for educational and entertainment purposes only. It is not intended to be a substitute for professional advice or judgment. Readers are encouraged to conduct their own research and to seek professional advice where appropriate. Every effort has been made to obtain necessary permissions and acknowledgments for all images and other copyrighted material used in this book. Any errors or omissions in this regard are unintentional, and the author and publisher will correct them in future editions.

BOOK 1 - RHCSA EXAM PASS: FOUNDATIONS OF LINUX ADMINISTRATION

BOOK 2 - RHCSA EXAM PASS: ADVANCED SYSTEM CONFIGURATION AND MANAGEMENT

BOOK 3 - RHCSA EXAM PASS: NETWORK ADMINISTRATION AND SECURITY

BOOK 4 - RHCSA EXAM PASS: PERFORMANCE TUNING AND TROUBLESHOOTING TECHNIQUES

Introduction

Welcome to the "RHCSA Exam Pass" book bundle, your comprehensive guide to becoming a Red Hat Certified System Administrator (RHCSA). In today's dynamic IT landscape, proficiency in Linux system administration is essential for success, and obtaining the RHCSA certification validates your expertise and opens doors to exciting career opportunities. This book bundle consists of four carefully crafted volumes, each designed to cover key areas of Linux administration and prepare you thoroughly for the RHCSA exam.

Book 1, "RHCSA Exam Pass: Foundations of Linux Administration," serves as your starting point on the journey to RHCSA certification. Here, you will explore fundamental concepts such as file system navigation, user and group management, permissions, and basic shell scripting. Whether you are new to Linux or looking to solidify your understanding of core concepts, this book will lay a strong foundation for your learning.

Building upon the foundational knowledge gained in Book 1, "RHCSA Exam Pass: Advanced System Configuration and Management" delves into more complex system configuration topics. From service management with systemd to disk partitioning, file system optimization, and repository configuration, this volume equips you with the skills needed to manage sophisticated Linux environments effectively.

Book 3, "RHCSA Exam Pass: Network Administration and Security," explores the critical aspects of network configuration, DNS, DHCP, firewalls, VPNs, and security measures. In today's interconnected world, securing network infrastructures is paramount, and this book will empower you to design, configure, and maintain secure networks in a Red Hat environment.

Finally, in Book 4, "RHCSA Exam Pass: Performance Tuning and Troubleshooting Techniques," you will learn how to optimize system performance and troubleshoot common issues. From analyzing system logs and monitoring performance metrics to identifying and resolving performance bottlenecks, this volume will help you ensure the health and efficiency of your Linux systems.

Whether you are a seasoned Linux professional seeking to validate your skills with certification or an aspiring system administrator looking to enter the field, the "RHCSA Exam Pass" book bundle provides the comprehensive coverage and hands-on exercises you need to succeed. With its structured approach and real-world scenarios, this bundle is your ultimate resource for mastering Linux administration and achieving RHCSA certification. Let's embark on this learning journey together and unlock new opportunities in the world of Linux system administration.

BOOK 1

RHCSA EXAM PASS

FOUNDATIONS OF LINUX ADMINISTRATION

ROB BOTWRIGHT

Chapter 1: Introduction to Linux Operating System

Linux, a Unix-like operating system kernel, was created by Linus Torvalds in 1991 as a hobby project while he was a student at the University of Helsinki, Finland. It initially started as a personal project, but soon attracted attention from other developers around the world who contributed to its development. The Linux kernel was inspired by Unix, an operating system developed at Bell Labs in the late 1960s. Unix had a powerful and stable design, but it was proprietary and expensive. Torvalds aimed to create a Unix-like system that was freely available and could run on personal computers. The development of Linux was facilitated by the GNU Project, launched in 1983 by Richard Stallman, which aimed to create a complete Unix-like operating system composed entirely of free software. While the GNU Project provided many essential tools and utilities for a Unix-like system, it lacked a kernel. Linux filled this gap, combining with the GNU utilities to create what is now known as the GNU/Linux operating system. Linux quickly gained popularity among developers and enthusiasts due to its open-source nature, flexibility, and stability. The open-source model allowed anyone to view, modify, and distribute the source code, fostering collaboration and innovation. Throughout the 1990s, Linux continued to evolve, with contributions from thousands of developers worldwide. Major corporations also began to adopt Linux for servers and embedded systems due to its reliability and cost-effectiveness. In 1998, the Open Source Initiative (OSI) was founded to promote open-source software development and advocate for the principles of open-source licensing. The OSI defined the term "open source" and created the Open Source Definition, which outlines criteria for software to be considered open source. Linux distributions, or "distros," emerged as collections of the Linux kernel, GNU utilities, and additional software packaged together for easy installation and use. Some popular Linux distributions include Debian, Ubuntu, Fedora, and CentOS. Each distribution may have its own package management system, configuration tools, and default desktop environment, catering to different user preferences and needs. Over the years, Linux has expanded beyond traditional computing platforms to power a wide range of devices, including servers, smartphones, embedded systems, and supercomputers. The Android operating system, based on the Linux kernel, dominates the mobile device market, while Linux is also prevalent in the server market, running a significant portion of internet servers worldwide. The development of Linux is driven by a global community of developers, companies, and organizations who collaborate to improve the kernel and create new features. The Linux Foundation, founded in 2007, plays a crucial role in fostering collaboration and supporting the development of Linux and other open-source projects. It provides resources, infrastructure, and governance for various open-source initiatives, including the Linux kernel development. The Linux kernel itself continues to evolve with regular releases, incorporating new features, performance improvements, and security enhancements. Developers contribute patches and new features to the kernel through mailing lists, code repositories, and collaborative platforms like GitHub. The development process follows a meritocratic model, where contributions are evaluated based on their technical merit and benefit to the kernel. Linus Torvalds remains the maintainer of the Linux kernel, overseeing the release cycle and making the final decisions on which patches are accepted. The success of Linux can be attributed to its strong community, open development model, and technical excellence. It has become a cornerstone of the modern computing landscape, powering critical infrastructure, driving innovation, and empowering users around the world. As Linux continues to evolve and adapt to new technologies and use cases, its impact on the world of computing is likely to grow even further. Linux distributions, also known as distros, are diverse and varied operating systems built on the Linux kernel and typically include a collection of software packages tailored for specific purposes or user groups. Debian, one of the oldest and most respected Linux distributions, is known for its stability, adherence to free software principles, and extensive package repositories. Ubuntu, a popular derivative of Debian, is known for its user-friendly interface and focus on usability, making it a favorite among desktop users. Fedora, sponsored by Red Hat, is a cutting-edge distribution that showcases the latest open-source technologies and serves as a testing ground for future features of Red Hat Enterprise Linux (RHEL). CentOS, also sponsored by Red Hat, is a community-driven distribution known for its stability and long-term support, making it a popular choice for servers. Arch Linux, known for its simplicity and flexibility, follows a rolling release model, allowing users to receive the latest updates continuously. Gentoo, a source-based distribution, offers a high degree of customization and optimization by compiling packages from source code. Slackware, one of the oldest surviving Linux distributions, maintains a traditional Unix-like approach with simplicity and stability as its core principles. Each Linux distribution has its own package management system to install, update, and remove software packages. Debian-based distributions, including Ubuntu and Linux Mint, use the Advanced Package Tool (APT) to manage software packages from centralized repositories. The APT command-line tool provides commands such as apt-get and aptitude for package management tasks, including installing, upgrading, and removing packages. Red Hat-based distributions, such as Fedora, CentOS, and RHEL, use the Yellowdog Updater, Modified (YUM) or its successor DNF (Dandified YUM) as the package management system. The yum command is used to manage software packages, repositories, and dependencies. Additionally, Red Hat distributions support RPM (Red Hat Package Manager) packages, which can be installed directly using the rpm command. Arch Linux, known for its simplicity and minimalism, uses the Pacman package manager, which provides commands like pacman -S to install packages and pacman -Syu to update the system. Gentoo, being a source-based distribution, uses the Portage package management system, which compiles packages from source code based on ebuild scripts. Slackware, following a more traditional approach, relies on simple shell scripts for package management tasks and does not have a dedicated package manager. Instead, users manually download and install packages or use third-party package managers like slapt-get or sbopkg. In addition to the mainstream distributions, there are also specialized Linux distributions tailored for specific purposes or user groups. For example, Kali Linux is designed for penetration testing and cybersecurity professionals, providing a wide range of security tools out-of-the-box. Tails is a privacy-focused distribution that aims to preserve anonymity and security by running entirely from a USB stick without leaving any trace on the host system. Linux distributions are available for a wide range of hardware architectures, including x86, ARM, and PowerPC, making them suitable for various devices, from desktop computers to embedded systems and servers. The choice of Linux distribution depends on factors such as user preference, intended use case, hardware compatibility, and support requirements. While some users prefer the familiarity and ease of use of mainstream distributions like Ubuntu or Fedora, others may opt for the flexibility and customization options offered by distributions like Arch Linux or Gentoo. Ultimately, the vast ecosystem of Linux distributions caters to the diverse needs and preferences of users worldwide, contributing to the popularity and widespread adoption of the Linux operating system.

Chapter 2: Understanding Linux File System Hierarchy

The directory structure of a Linux system provides a hierarchical organization of files and directories, facilitating efficient file management and system administration tasks. At the root of the directory hierarchy is the root directory, denoted by '/'. Beneath the root directory are several essential system directories, each serving a specific purpose. The '/bin' directory contains essential binary executables, such as system utilities and commands required for basic system functionality. Common commands like 'ls', 'cp', and 'mv' reside in this directory, allowing users to perform fundamental file management tasks. The '/sbin' directory holds binary executables primarily used by system administrators for system maintenance and configuration tasks. Commands in this directory typically require elevated privileges to execute, as they are used for system administration purposes. Examples include 'ifconfig' for network configuration and 'fdisk' for disk partitioning. The '/usr' directory contains user-related files and programs, including user binaries, libraries, documentation, and shared data used by applications. Within '/usr', the '/bin' and '/sbin' directories are mirrored, containing non-essential system binaries and administrative commands, respectively. The '/usr/bin' directory houses user commands and executables that are not essential for system boot or repair but are commonly used by regular users. Similarly, the '/usr/sbin' directory contains administrative commands and utilities used by system administrators. The '/usr/local' directory is reserved for locally-installed software and user-specific programs not provided by the operating system's package manager. It serves as a location for installing custom applications or software packages that are not part of the standard distribution. The '/etc' directory contains system-wide configuration files used by various applications and services. Configuration files in '/etc' govern system behavior and settings, such as network configuration ('/etc/network/interfaces') and user account information ('/etc/passwd' and '/etc/group'). The '/var' directory holds variable data files, including logs, spool files, temporary files, and other frequently-changing data generated by system processes and applications. Log files from system services are stored in '/var/log', while printer spool files reside in '/var/spool'. The '/tmp' directory provides a location for temporary files created by users or system processes. Files in '/tmp' are typically short-lived and may be deleted upon system reboot or periodically by system maintenance scripts. The '/dev' directory contains device files representing physical and virtual devices attached to the system. Device files in '/dev' provide an interface for interacting with hardware components and peripheral devices. For example, '/dev/sda' represents the first SCSI or SATA disk drive, while '/dev/null' is a special device file used for discarding output. The '/proc' directory is a virtual filesystem that provides access to kernel and process information in real-time. It contains directories and files representing system resources, hardware configurations, and running processes. Information in '/proc' can be accessed and manipulated using standard file system operations and commands. The '/boot' directory contains files required for system booting, including the kernel image, initial ramdisk ('initrd' or 'initramfs'), and boot loader configuration files. The kernel image ('vmlinuz') and initial ramdisk are essential for the initial stages of the boot process, loading necessary drivers and modules to mount the root file system. The '/home' directory is the default location for user home directories, where users store their personal files and configuration settings. Each user typically has a subdirectory within '/home' named after their username, such as '/home/user1' or '/home/user2'. User-specific configuration files and data are stored within their respective home directories. The '/root' directory is the home directory for the 'root' user, also known as the superuser or system administrator. Unlike regular user home directories, which reside in '/home', the root user's home directory is located at '/root'. It contains configuration files, scripts, and other system-related data specific to the root user. The directory structure of a Linux system provides a standardized layout that facilitates system administration, software installation, and file management tasks. Understanding the purpose and organization of key directories is essential for navigating the file system, locating files and configuration settings, and effectively managing the system's resources. With knowledge of the directory structure, users and administrators can navigate the file system with ease, locate files and directories quickly, and perform system maintenance and troubleshooting tasks efficiently.

File system navigation commands are essential tools for navigating and exploring the directory structure of a Linux system, allowing users to view, manipulate, and manage files and directories from the command line. One of the most commonly used file system navigation commands is 'ls', which lists the contents of a directory, displaying file names, permissions, ownership, and other attributes. By typing 'ls' followed by the name of a directory, users can view its contents, and adding options such as '-l' provides detailed information about each file and directory. For example, 'ls -l /home' displays a long listing of the files and directories in the '/home' directory. Another useful navigation command is 'cd', which stands for "change directory". The 'cd' command allows users to navigate between directories by specifying the desired directory path as an argument. For instance, typing 'cd /var/log' changes the current directory to '/var/log'. Additionally, using 'cd' without any arguments takes the user to their home directory. To move up one directory level, users can type 'cd ..', and to move to the previous directory, they can use 'cd -'. 'pwd' is a command used to print the current working directory, displaying the full path of the directory the user is currently in. It is particularly useful when working with complex directory structures or when needing to reference the current directory path. 'mkdir' is used to create new directories within the file system. By typing 'mkdir' followed by the name of the new directory, users can create a directory in the current working directory. For example, 'mkdir documents' creates a new directory named 'documents' in the current directory. To remove directories, the 'rmdir' command is used. However, 'rmdir' only works on empty directories. If a directory contains files or other directories, the 'rm' command is used with the '-r' option to recursively remove all contents within the directory. For example, 'rm -r documents' deletes the 'documents' directory and all its contents. 'mv' is a command used to move or rename files and directories. By specifying the source file or directory followed by the destination, users can move files to a different directory or rename them. For instance, 'mv file1.txt directory1/' moves 'file1.txt' to 'directory1', while 'mv file1.txt file2.txt' renames 'file1.txt' to 'file2.txt'. 'cp' is used to copy files and directories. Similar to 'mv', users specify the source file or directory followed by the destination. For example, 'cp file1.txt directory1/' copies 'file1.txt' to 'directory1', while 'cp -r directory1/ directory2/' copies 'directory1' and its contents to 'directory2'. 'touch' is a command used to create empty files or update file timestamps. By typing 'touch' followed by the name of the file, users can create a new empty file in the current directory. For example, 'touch newfile.txt' creates a new empty file named 'newfile.txt'. 'rm' is used to remove files and directories from the file system. When used with the '-rf' options, it can recursively remove directories and their contents forcefully. However, caution should be exercised when using 'rm -rf', as it permanently deletes files and directories without confirmation. For example, 'rm file1.txt' deletes 'file1.txt' from the file system. The 'find' command is used to search for files and directories within a specified directory hierarchy based on various criteria such as name, size, or permissions. By typing 'find' followed by the directory to search and the search criteria, users can locate files matching specific patterns or attributes. For example, 'find /home -name "*.txt"' searches the '/home' directory for files with a '.txt' extension. 'grep' is a powerful command-line utility used to search for patterns within text files. By typing 'grep' followed by the search pattern and the file to search, users can locate lines containing the specified pattern. For example, 'grep "keyword" file.txt' searches 'file.txt' for lines containing the word "keyword". These file system navigation commands provide users with the flexibility and efficiency to manage files and directories from the command line effectively. Whether listing directory contents, navigating between directories, creating, moving, or deleting files, or searching for specific files and patterns within text files, these commands form the foundation of file system navigation and manipulation in Linux. By mastering these commands, users can streamline their workflow, increase productivity, and effectively manage their file systems with confidence.

Chapter 3: Command Line Basics: Navigating and File Management

Working with files and directories is a fundamental aspect of managing a Linux system, and mastering the various command-line tools available for this purpose is essential for efficient system administration and everyday tasks. One of the most basic commands for interacting with files and directories is 'ls', which stands for "list". By typing 'ls' followed by the name of a directory, users can list the contents of that directory, providing a quick overview of the files and subdirectories it contains. Additionally, using the '-l' option with 'ls' displays a detailed listing that includes additional information such as file permissions, ownership, size, and modification date. For example, 'ls -l /home/user' lists the contents of the '/home/user' directory in long format. 'cd', short for "change directory", is used to navigate between directories. By typing 'cd' followed by the name of the directory, users can change their current working directory to the specified location. For instance, 'cd /var/log' changes the current directory to '/var/log'. Typing 'cd' without any arguments takes the user to their home directory. To move up one directory level, users can type 'cd ..', and to move to the previous directory, they can use 'cd -'. 'pwd', which stands for "print working directory", displays the full path of the current working directory. This command is particularly useful when working with complex directory structures or when needing to reference the current directory path. By typing 'pwd', users can quickly determine their current location within the file system. Another essential command for working with files and directories is 'mkdir', which is used to create new directories. By typing 'mkdir' followed by the name of the new directory, users can create a directory in the current working directory. For example, 'mkdir documents' creates a new directory named 'documents' in the current directory. 'rmdir' is used to remove empty directories from the file system. If a directory contains files or other directories, the 'rm' command is used with the '-r' option to recursively remove all contents within the directory. For instance, 'rm -r documents' deletes the 'documents' directory and all its contents. 'mv' is a command used to move or rename files and directories. By specifying the source file or directory followed by the destination, users can move files to a different directory or rename them. For example, 'mv file1.txt directory1/' moves 'file1.txt' to 'directory1', while 'mv file1.txt file2.txt' renames 'file1.txt' to 'file2.txt'. 'cp', short for "copy", is used to copy files and directories. Similar to 'mv', users specify the source file or directory followed by the destination. For example, 'cp file1.txt directory1/' copies 'file1.txt' to 'directory1', while 'cp -r directory1/ directory2/' copies 'directory1' and its contents to 'directory2'. 'touch' is used to create empty files or update file timestamps. By typing 'touch' followed by the name of the file, users can create a new empty file in the current directory. For example, 'touch newfile.txt' creates a new empty file named 'newfile.txt'. 'rm' is used to remove files and directories from the file system. When used with the '-rf' options, it can recursively remove directories and their contents forcefully. However, caution should be exercised when using 'rm -rf', as it permanently deletes files and directories without confirmation. For example, 'rm file1.txt' deletes 'file1.txt' from the file system. 'find' is a command used to search for files and directories within a specified directory hierarchy based on various criteria such as name, size, or permissions. By typing 'find' followed by the directory to search and the search criteria, users can locate files matching specific patterns or attributes. For example, 'find /home -name

"*.txt"' searches the '/home' directory for files with a '.txt' extension. 'grep', another powerful command-line utility, is used to search for patterns within text files. By typing 'grep' followed by the search pattern and the file to search, users can locate lines containing the specified pattern. For example, 'grep "keyword" file.txt' searches 'file.txt' for lines containing the word "keyword". These file and directory manipulation commands provide users with the flexibility and efficiency to manage files and directories from the command line effectively. Whether listing directory contents, navigating between directories, creating, moving, copying, or deleting files and directories, or searching for specific files and patterns within text files, these commands form the foundation of file and directory management in Linux. By mastering these commands, users can streamline their workflow, increase productivity, and effectively manage their file systems with confidence. Command Line Wildcards and Redirection are powerful features of the command-line interface in Linux, providing users with efficient ways to manipulate and process files and text. Wildcards are special characters used to represent one or more characters in a file name or pattern, allowing users to perform operations on multiple files simultaneously. The '*' wildcard, also known as the asterisk, matches any sequence of characters, including none. For example, 'ls *.txt' lists all files with a '.txt' extension in the current directory. Similarly, 'cp *.txt directory/' copies all files with a '.txt' extension to the 'directory' directory. The '?' wildcard matches any single character, useful for specifying files with similar names differing by one character. For instance, 'ls file?.txt' lists files like 'file1.txt', 'file2.txt', but not 'file10.txt'. The '[ ]' wildcard, also known as character classes or ranges, matches any single character within the specified range or list. For example, 'ls file[1-3].txt' lists files like 'file1.txt', 'file2.txt', and 'file3.txt'. Multiple ranges or characters can be specified within the brackets, such as 'ls file[1-3ab].txt'. Additionally, the '[!]' wildcard matches any character not within the specified range or list. Redirection is another essential feature of the command-line interface, allowing users to control the input and output of commands. The '>' operator redirects command output to a file, overwriting its contents if it already exists or creating a new file if it does not. For instance, 'ls > files.txt' redirects the output of the 'ls' command to a file named 'files.txt'. If 'files.txt' already exists, its contents are overwritten. To append command output to a file without overwriting its contents, the '>>'

operator is used. For example, 'ls >> files.txt' appends the output of the 'ls' command to the end of the 'files.txt' file. The '<' operator redirects input from a file to a command, allowing users to use file contents as input for commands. For instance, 'sort < input.txt' sorts the lines of the 'input.txt' file and displays the result in the terminal. Additionally, pipes ('|') can be used to redirect the output of one command as input to another command. For example, 'ls | grep "pattern"' lists files in the current directory and filters the output to display only those containing the specified pattern. Redirection and wildcards can be combined to perform complex operations efficiently. For example, 'grep "keyword" *.txt > results.txt' searches for the specified keyword in all '.txt' files in the current directory and redirects the matching lines to a file named 'results.txt'. Similarly, 'cat *.log | grep "error" > error.log' concatenates the contents of all '.log' files in the current directory, filters the output to display only lines containing the word "error", and redirects the result to a file named 'error.log'. Understanding and mastering wildcards and redirection are essential skills for Linux users, enabling them to perform a wide range of tasks efficiently from the command line. Whether searching for files, processing text, or managing command output, wildcards and redirection provide powerful tools for navigating and manipulating the file system and executing commands with precision and control. By incorporating wildcards and redirection into their command-line workflows, users can streamline their tasks, automate repetitive processes, and maximize their productivity in the Linux environment.

Chapter 4: User and Group Management

User account creation and management are fundamental tasks in Linux system administration, allowing administrators to grant access to resources, manage permissions, and enforce security policies. The 'adduser' command is commonly used to create new user accounts on a Linux system. By typing 'adduser' followed by the username, administrators can create a new user account interactively, specifying details such as the user's full name, home directory, and initial group membership. For example, 'adduser john' prompts the administrator to set up the account for the user named 'john', including setting a password and creating a home directory. Alternatively, the 'useradd' command can be used to create new user accounts non-interactively from the command line. By typing 'useradd' followed by the username, administrators can create a new user account with default settings. For instance, 'useradd -m -s /bin/bash jessica' creates a new user account named 'jessica' with a home directory and the Bash shell as the default login shell. After creating a user account, administrators can set or change the user's password using the 'passwd' command. By typing 'passwd' followed by the username, administrators can prompt the user to set or change their password. For example, 'passwd john' allows the user named 'john' to change their password. Additionally, administrators can use the 'chage' command to set password expiration and aging policies for user accounts. By typing 'chage' followed by the username, administrators can configure settings such as password expiration dates, minimum and maximum password ages, and password warning periods. For instance, 'chage -M 90 john' sets the maximum password age for the user named 'john' to 90 days. User accounts can be assigned to one or more groups to control access permissions and manage resource sharing. The 'usermod' command is used to modify user account properties, including group membership. By typing 'usermod -aG' followed by the group name and username, administrators can add a user to an additional group. For example, 'usermod -aG developers john' adds the user named 'john' to the 'developers' group. Conversely, the 'deluser' command is used to delete user accounts from the system. By typing 'deluser' followed by the username, administrators can remove a user account and optionally delete the user's home directory and mail spool. For instance, 'deluser --remove-home john' deletes the user account named 'john' and removes their home directory. Administrators can manage user account properties and permissions using the 'usermod' command. By typing 'usermod' followed by various options, administrators can modify user account properties such as the home directory, login shell, and account expiration date. For example, 'usermod -d /home/newhome -s /bin/sh john' changes the home directory of the user named 'john' to '/home/newhome' and sets the login shell to '/bin/sh'. Additionally, administrators can lock or unlock user accounts using the 'usermod' command. By typing 'usermod -L' followed by the username, administrators can lock a user account, preventing the user from logging in. Conversely, 'usermod -U' unlocks a locked user account, allowing the user to log in again. For example, 'usermod -L john' locks the user account named 'john', while 'usermod -U john' unlocks it. User account management is an essential aspect of Linux system administration, enabling administrators to control access to resources, enforce security policies, and manage user privileges effectively. By mastering the various commands and techniques for creating, modifying, and deleting user accounts, administrators can ensure the security and integrity of their Linux systems while providing users with the necessary access to perform their tasks efficiently.

Group creation and permissions are integral components of Linux system administration, facilitating efficient management of access control and resource sharing among users. The 'groupadd' command is commonly used to create new groups on a Linux system. By typing 'groupadd' followed by the group name, administrators can create a new group. For example, 'groupadd developers' creates a new group named 'developers'. Additionally, administrators can use the 'gpasswd' command to manage group membership and set group passwords. By typing 'gpasswd' followed by the group name, administrators can add or remove users from the group. For instance, 'gpasswd -a john developers' adds the user named 'john' to the 'developers' group. Group permissions play a crucial role in controlling access to files and directories on a Linux system. Each file and directory is associated with a set of permissions that determine who can read, write, or execute the file. The 'chmod' command is used to modify file permissions, allowing administrators to grant or revoke permissions for users, groups, and others. By typing 'chmod' followed by the permission mode and file name, administrators can change the permissions of a file. For example, 'chmod u+r file.txt' adds read permission for the file owner, while 'chmod g-w file.txt' removes write permission for the group. In addition to modifying permissions individually, administrators can use symbolic notation or octal mode to set permissions more efficiently. Symbolic notation allows administrators to specify permissions symbolically using letters ('u' for user, 'g' for group, 'o' for others) and symbols ('+' for adding permissions, '-' for removing permissions, '=' for setting permissions explicitly). For example, 'chmod g+w file.txt' adds write permission for the group, while 'chmod o-rwx file.txt' removes read, write, and execute permissions for others. Octal mode allows administrators to specify permissions numerically using a three-digit code, where each digit represents the permissions for the owner, group, and others, respectively. For instance, 'chmod 644 file.txt' sets read and write permissions for the owner and read-only permissions for the group and others. In addition to setting file permissions, administrators can use the 'chown' command to change the ownership of files and directories. By typing 'chown' followed by the new owner and file name, administrators can transfer ownership of a file. For example, 'chown john file.txt' changes the owner of 'file.txt' to the user named 'john'. Additionally, administrators can use the 'chgrp' command to change the group ownership of files and directories. By typing 'chgrp' followed by the new group and file name, administrators can transfer group ownership of a file. For instance, 'chgrp developers file.txt' changes the group owner of 'file.txt' to the 'developers' group. Linux systems use a set of default permissions for newly created files and directories, known as umask. The 'umask' command is used to set or display the umask value, which specifies the permissions that are not granted by default. By typing 'umask' followed by the desired umask value, administrators can configure the default permissions for new files and directories. For example, 'umask 022' sets the default permissions to 'rw-r--r--' for files and 'rwxr-xr-x' for directories. Group creation and permissions management are essential tasks for Linux system administrators, enabling effective control of access to resources and ensuring proper collaboration among users. By utilizing commands such as 'groupadd', 'gpasswd', 'chmod', 'chown', and 'chgrp', administrators can create and manage groups, set file permissions, and control ownership of files and directories with precision and efficiency. Understanding and mastering group creation and permissions management are critical skills for Linux system administrators, allowing them to maintain the security and integrity of their systems while facilitating seamless collaboration and resource sharing among users.

Chapter 5: Permissions and Ownership in Linux

Understanding file permissions is crucial for effectively managing access control and security on a Linux system, as they determine who can read, write, or execute files and directories. Each file and directory in a Linux system is associated with three sets of permissions: one for the owner, one for the group, and one for others. The 'ls -l' command displays detailed information about files and directories, including their permissions. For example, 'ls -l file.txt' shows the permissions of the file 'file.txt'. File permissions are represented by a 10-character string, where the first character indicates the file type ('-' for a regular file, 'd' for a directory, 'l' for a symbolic link, and others for special files), and the next nine characters represent the permissions for the owner, group, and others. The three sets of permissions consist of three characters each, indicating read ('r'), write ('w'), and execute ('x') permissions, respectively. If a permission is granted, the corresponding character is displayed; otherwise, a hyphen '-' is shown. For example, 'rw-r--r--' indicates that the owner has read and write permissions, while the group and others have only read permissions. To modify file permissions, the 'chmod' command is used. By typing 'chmod' followed by the desired permission mode and file name, users can change the permissions of a file. Permission modes can be specified symbolically using letters ('u' for user, 'g' for group, 'o' for others) and symbols ('+' for adding permissions, '-' for removing permissions, '=' for setting permissions explicitly). For example, 'chmod u+x file.txt' adds execute permission for the owner, while 'chmod g-w file.txt' removes write permission for the group. Alternatively, permission modes can be specified numerically using a three-digit code, where each digit represents the permissions for the owner, group, and others, respectively. For instance, 'chmod 755 file.txt' sets read, write, and execute permissions for the owner, and read and execute permissions for the group and others. File permissions can also be set using octal notation, where each permission is represented by a numeric value: 4 for read, 2 for write, and 1 for execute. These values are then added together to determine the permission mode. For example, 'chmod 644 file.txt' sets read and write permissions for the owner, and read-only permissions for the group and others. In addition to setting file permissions, the 'chown' command is used to change the

ownership of files and directories. By typing 'chown' followed by the new owner and file name, users can transfer ownership of a file. For example, 'chown john file.txt' changes the owner of 'file.txt' to the user named 'john'. Similarly, the 'chgrp' command is used to change the group ownership of files and directories. By typing 'chgrp' followed by the new group and file name, users can transfer group ownership of a file. For instance, 'chgrp developers file.txt' changes the group owner of 'file.txt' to the 'developers' group. File permissions play a crucial role in controlling access to files and directories on a Linux system, ensuring data security and integrity. By understanding how to interpret and modify file permissions using commands like 'ls', 'chmod', 'chown', and 'chgrp', users can effectively manage access control and enforce security policies on their systems. Whether granting specific permissions to individual users, groups, or others, or setting default permissions for newly created files and directories, mastering file permissions is essential for maintaining a secure and well-organized Linux environment.
Modifying file permissions and ownership is a fundamental aspect of managing access control and security on a Linux system, enabling administrators to tailor permissions and

ownership settings to meet specific requirements. The 'chmod' command is the primary tool used to modify file permissions, allowing users to grant or revoke read, write, and execute permissions for the owner, group, and others. By typing 'chmod' followed by the desired permission mode and file name, users can change the permissions of a file. Permission modes can be specified symbolically using letters ('u' for user, 'g' for group, 'o' for others) and symbols ('+' for adding permissions, '-' for removing permissions, '=' for setting permissions explicitly). For example, 'chmod u+x file.txt' adds execute permission for the owner, while 'chmod g-w file.txt' removes write permission for the group. Alternatively, permission modes can be specified numerically using a three-digit code, where each digit represents the permissions for the owner, group, and others, respectively. For instance, 'chmod 755 file.txt' sets read, write, and execute permissions for the owner, and read and execute permissions for the group and others. File ownership can be changed using the 'chown' command, which allows users to transfer ownership of a file to another user or group. By typing 'chown' followed by the new owner and file name, users can change the owner of a file. For example, 'chown john file.txt' changes the owner of 'file.txt' to the user named 'john'. Similarly, the 'chgrp' command is used to change the group ownership of files and directories. By typing 'chgrp' followed by the new group and file name, users can transfer group ownership of a file. For instance, 'chgrp developers file.txt' changes the group owner of 'file.txt' to the 'developers' group. Understanding and mastering file permissions and ownership are essential for ensuring data security and integrity on a Linux system. Administrators must carefully consider which users and groups require access to specific files and directories and adjust permissions and ownership settings accordingly. Additionally, administrators should regularly audit file permissions and ownership to identify and address any security vulnerabilities or misconfigurations. By using commands like 'chmod', 'chown', and 'chgrp', administrators can effectively manage access control and enforce security policies to protect sensitive data and resources from unauthorized access or modification. Whether granting specific permissions to individual users or groups, transferring ownership of files and directories, or setting default permissions for newly created files, mastering file permissions and ownership management is essential for maintaining a secure and well-organized Linux environment.

Chapter 6: Package Management: Installing and Updating Software

Package managers play a pivotal role in the management of software on Linux systems, facilitating the installation, update, and removal of software packages while managing dependencies and ensuring system integrity. There are several package managers available for different Linux distributions, each with its own set of commands and features. One of the most widely used package managers is 'apt' (Advanced Package Tool), which is used on Debian-based distributions such as Ubuntu. The 'apt' command is used to perform package management operations, including installing, updating, and removing packages. For example, 'apt install package_name' installs a package, 'apt update' updates the package index to ensure it is up-to-date, and 'apt remove package_name' removes a package. Another popular package manager is 'yum' (Yellowdog Updater Modified), used on RPM-based distributions such as Red Hat Enterprise Linux (RHEL) and CentOS. The 'yum' command is used to manage software packages and dependencies, similar to 'apt'. For example, 'yum install package_name' installs a package, 'yum update' updates all installed packages, and 'yum remove package_name' removes a package. In recent years, 'yum' has been replaced by 'dnf' (Dandified Yum) as the default package manager on newer versions of RHEL and CentOS. 'dnf' offers improved performance and additional features compared to 'yum' but retains similar syntax for package management operations. Another widely used package manager is 'pacman', which is used on Arch Linux and its derivatives. 'pacman' is a powerful package manager that allows users to install, update, and remove packages with ease. For example, 'pacman -S package_name' installs a package, 'pacman -Syu' updates all installed packages, and 'pacman -R package_name' removes a package. 'zypper' is the default package manager on openSUSE and SUSE Linux Enterprise Server (SLES). It is a command-line tool for managing software packages and repositories on SUSE-based distributions. For example, 'zypper install package_name' installs a package, 'zypper update' updates all installed packages, and 'zypper remove package_name' removes a package. These are just a few examples of the many package managers available for Linux distributions. Each package manager has its own set of commands and features, but they all serve the same purpose of simplifying the management of software packages and dependencies on Linux systems. Package managers automate the process of installing, updating, and removing software packages, saving users time and effort while ensuring system consistency and stability. They also handle dependency resolution, ensuring that all required libraries and dependencies are installed correctly when installing new software. Overall, package managers are essential tools for Linux system administrators and users alike, enabling efficient software management and ensuring a smooth and hassle-free user experience.

Installing, updating, and removing software packages are fundamental tasks in Linux system administration, allowing users to manage the software installed on their systems efficiently and keep it up-to-date. Package managers provide a convenient way to perform these operations, automating the process of software management and handling dependencies to ensure system integrity. One of the most commonly used package managers on Debian-based distributions such as Ubuntu is 'apt' (Advanced Package Tool). To install a software package using 'apt', users can use the 'apt install' command followed by the name of the package. For example, 'apt install firefox' installs the Firefox web browser. Updating software packages with 'apt' is done using the 'apt update' command, which refreshes the package index to ensure it is up-to-date, followed by 'apt upgrade' to install available updates. Removing software packages with 'apt' is straightforward using the 'apt remove' command followed by the name of the package. For instance, 'apt remove firefox' removes the Firefox web browser from the system. Another widely used package manager is 'yum' (Yellowdog Updater Modified), which is prevalent on RPM-based distributions such as Red Hat Enterprise Linux (RHEL) and CentOS. To install a software package using 'yum', users can use the 'yum install' command followed by the name of the package. For example, 'yum install nginx' installs the NGINX web server. Updating software packages with 'yum' is achieved using the 'yum update' command, which updates all installed packages to the latest versions. Removing software packages with 'yum' can be done using the 'yum remove' command followed by the name of the package. For instance, 'yum remove nginx' removes the NGINX web server from the system. In recent years, 'yum' has been replaced by 'dnf' (Dandified Yum) as the default package manager on newer versions of RHEL and CentOS. 'dnf' offers improved performance and additional features compared to 'yum' but retains similar syntax for package management operations. To install a software package using 'dnf', users can use the 'dnf install' command followed by the name of the package. For example, 'dnf install mariadb-server' installs the MariaDB database server. Updating software packages with 'dnf' is done using the 'dnf update' command, which updates all installed packages to the latest versions. Removing software packages with 'dnf' can be achieved using the 'dnf remove' command followed by the name of the package. For instance, 'dnf remove mariadb-server' removes the MariaDB database server from the system. 'pacman' is the default package manager on Arch Linux and its derivatives. To install a software package using 'pacman', users can use the 'pacman -S' command followed by the name of the package. For example, 'pacman -S vim' installs the Vim text editor. Updating software packages with 'pacman' is done using the 'pacman -Syu' command, which updates all installed packages to the latest versions. Removing software packages with 'pacman' is straightforward using the 'pacman -R' command followed by the name of the package. For instance, 'pacman -R vim' removes the Vim text editor from the system.

'zypper' is the default package manager on openSUSE and SUSE Linux Enterprise Server (SLES). To install a software package using 'zypper', users can use the 'zypper install' command followed by the name of the package. For example, 'zypper install apache2' installs the Apache web server. Updating software packages with 'zypper' is achieved using the 'zypper update' command, which updates all installed packages to the latest versions. Removing software packages with 'zypper' is done using the 'zypper remove' command followed by the name of the package. For instance, 'zypper remove apache2' removes the Apache web server from the system. These package managers provide users with efficient tools for installing, updating, and removing software packages on their Linux systems, enabling them to keep their systems up-to-date and secure while managing software dependencies effectively. Whether using 'apt', 'yum', 'dnf', 'pacman', or 'zypper', users can perform these operations with ease, ensuring that their systems are equipped with the latest software and security patches while maintaining system stability and integrity.

Chapter 7: Configuring Networking in Linux

Network configuration files and tools are essential components of Linux system administration, enabling users to manage network interfaces, IP addresses, routes, and other network settings effectively. One of the primary configuration files for network settings on Linux systems is '/etc/network/interfaces'. This file is used to configure network interfaces manually on Debian-based distributions such as Ubuntu. Users can edit this file using a text editor such as 'nano' or 'vim' to specify network settings such as IP address, netmask, gateway, and DNS servers for each interface. For instance, to configure a static IP address for the 'eth0' interface, users can add the following lines to the '/etc/network/interfaces' file: 'iface eth0 inet static', 'address 192.168.1.100', 'netmask 255.255.255.0', 'gateway 192.168.1.1', 'dns-nameservers 8.8.8.8 8.8.4.4'. On Red Hat-based distributions such as CentOS and Fedora, network configurations are typically managed using the 'nmcli' (Network Manager Command Line Interface) tool. 'nmcli' provides a command-line interface for managing NetworkManager, the default network management service on these distributions. Users can use 'nmcli' to view and modify network connections, devices, and settings. For example, to display information about all active network connections, users can run the 'nmcli connection show' command. To configure a static IP address for a network interface using 'nmcli', users can use the following command: 'nmcli connection modify eth0 ipv4.method manual ipv4.addresses 192.168.1.100/24 ipv4.gateway 192.168.1.1 ipv4.dns 8.8.8.8,8.8.4.4'. Another commonly used network configuration tool on Linux systems is 'ifconfig' (Interface Configuration). 'ifconfig' is a command-line utility that displays and configures network interfaces on a Linux system. Users can use 'ifconfig' to view information about network interfaces, configure IP addresses, enable or disable interfaces, and more. For example, to display information about all network interfaces, users can run the 'ifconfig' command without any arguments. To configure a network interface with a specific IP address and netmask, users can use the following command: 'ifconfig eth0 192.168.1.100 netmask 255.255.255.0'. However, 'ifconfig' has been deprecated on many Linux distributions in favor of newer tools such as 'ip' from the 'iproute2' package. 'ip' is a powerful command-line tool for managing network interfaces, addresses, routes, and more. Users can use 'ip' to perform various network configuration tasks, including displaying network interfaces, configuring IP addresses, adding routes, and managing network namespaces. For example, to display information about all network interfaces, users can run the 'ip link show' command. To configure a static IP address for a network interface using 'ip', users can use the following command: 'ip addr add 192.168.1.100/24 dev eth0'. In addition to these tools, users can also use configuration files such as '/etc/resolv.conf' to specify DNS server settings and '/etc/hosts' to configure hostname-to-IP address mappings. 'resolv.conf' is used to configure DNS resolver settings, including the IP addresses of DNS servers and search domains. Users can edit this file manually to specify DNS server IP addresses and search domains. For example, to specify Google's public DNS servers (8.8.8.8 and 8.8.4.4) as the DNS servers for the system, users can add the following lines to the '/etc/resolv.conf' file: 'nameserver 8.8.8.8', 'nameserver 8.8.4.4'. 'hosts' is used to map hostnames to IP addresses locally. Users can edit this file to add custom hostname-to-IP address mappings. For instance, to map the hostname 'example.com' to the IP address '192.168.1.100', users can add the following line to the '/etc/hosts' file: '192.168.1.100 example.com'. Overall, network configuration files and tools are essential for managing network settings on Linux systems, allowing users to configure network interfaces, IP addresses, routes, DNS servers, and more. Whether using configuration files such as '/etc/network/interfaces', '/etc/resolv.conf', and '/etc/hosts', or command-line tools such as 'nmcli', 'ifconfig', and 'ip', users have a variety of options for configuring and managing network settings to meet their specific requirements. Basic network troubleshooting commands are essential tools for diagnosing and resolving network issues on Linux systems, providing users with valuable information about network connectivity, configuration, and performance. One of the most commonly used network troubleshooting commands is 'ping', which is used to test network connectivity between two hosts. Users can use the 'ping' command followed by the IP address or hostname of the target host to send ICMP echo requests and receive ICMP echo replies. For example, 'ping google.com' sends ICMP echo requests to Google's DNS server and displays the round-trip time for each reply, allowing users to verify network connectivity to remote hosts. Another useful network troubleshooting command is 'traceroute', which is used to trace the route that packets take from the local host to a remote destination. Users can use the 'traceroute' command followed by the IP address or hostname of the target host to display a list of routers and the round-trip time for each hop along the path to the destination. For example, 'traceroute google.com' traces the route to Google's DNS server, showing the IP addresses of routers along the path and the time taken for each hop, helping users identify network bottlenecks or routing issues. 'netstat' is another valuable network troubleshooting command that provides information about network connections, routing tables, interface statistics, and more. Users can use the 'netstat' command with various options to display different types of network information. For example, 'netstat -tuln' displays a list of all listening TCP and UDP ports on the system, while 'netstat -r' displays the kernel routing table, showing the routes that packets take to reach different networks. The 'ip' command from the 'iproute2' package is a powerful tool for network configuration and troubleshooting. Users can use the 'ip' command with various subcommands to display and manipulate network interfaces, addresses, routes, and more. For example, 'ip addr show' displays information about all network interfaces on the system, including their IP addresses and status. 'ip route show' displays the kernel routing table, showing the routes that packets take to reach different networks, while 'ip neigh show' displays the neighbor cache, showing the IP and MAC addresses of neighboring devices on the local network segment. 'ss' is a replacement for the 'netstat' command that provides similar functionality but with better performance and more features. Users can use the 'ss' command with various options to display information about network connections, sockets, and more. For example, 'ss -tuln' displays a list of all listening TCP and UDP ports on the system, similar to 'netstat -tuln'. 'dig' (Domain Information Groper) is a command-line tool for querying DNS servers and retrieving DNS information such as IP addresses, MX records, and more. Users can use the 'dig' command followed by the domain name to perform DNS queries and retrieve information about the domain. For example, 'dig google.com' retrieves the IP addresses of Google's DNS servers, allowing users to verify DNS resolution and diagnose DNS-related issues. 'nslookup' is another command-line tool for querying DNS servers and retrieving DNS information. Users can use the 'nslookup' command followed by the domain name to perform DNS queries and retrieve information about the domain. For example, 'nslookup google.com' retrieves the IP addresses of Google's DNS servers, similar to the 'dig' command. In addition to these commands, users can also use utilities such as 'tcpdump' and 'wireshark' for network troubleshooting. 'tcpdump' is a command-line packet analyzer that captures and displays network packets in real-time, allowing users to inspect network traffic and diagnose network-related issues. For example, 'tcpdump -i eth0' captures packets on the 'eth0' network interface and displays information about each packet, including source and destination IP addresses, ports, and protocol. 'wireshark' is a graphical packet analyzer that provides similar functionality to 'tcpdump' but with a user-friendly interface. Users can use 'wireshark' to capture and analyze network packets in real-time, allowing them to troubleshoot network issues visually and interactively. Overall, basic network troubleshooting commands are indispensable tools for diagnosing and resolving network issues on Linux systems, providing users with valuable information about network connectivity, configuration, and performance. Whether using commands such as 'ping', 'traceroute', 'netstat', 'ip', 'ss', 'dig', or 'nslookup', users have a variety of options for troubleshooting network problems and ensuring smooth and reliable network operation.

Chapter 8: Essential System Services: Introduction and Configuration

System services are essential components of a Linux operating system, responsible for managing various aspects of system functionality, including network services, daemons, and background processes. One of the fundamental commands for managing system services on Linux systems is 'systemctl', which is used to control the systemd system and service manager. Users can use the 'systemctl' command with various options to manage system services, including starting, stopping, restarting, enabling, disabling, and checking the status of services. For example, 'systemctl start sshd' starts the SSH (Secure Shell) service, allowing remote users to connect to the system securely, while 'systemctl stop sshd' stops the SSH service, terminating existing connections. 'systemctl restart sshd' restarts the SSH service, reloading its configuration and applying any changes, while 'systemctl enable sshd' enables the SSH service to start automatically at system boot, ensuring continuous availability. Conversely, 'systemctl disable sshd' disables the SSH service from starting automatically at boot, providing users with control over which services are running on their systems. Another useful command for managing system services is 'service', which is a legacy command-line interface for controlling system services. While 'service' is still available on many Linux distributions, it is recommended to use 'systemctl' for managing services on systems that use systemd. Users can use the 'service' command with various options to perform actions such as starting, stopping, restarting, and checking the status of services. For example, 'service apache2 start' starts the Apache HTTP Server service, allowing users to host websites and web applications, while 'service apache2 stop' stops the Apache service, preventing access to hosted content. 'service apache2 restart' restarts the Apache service, reloading its configuration and applying any changes, ensuring uninterrupted service. Additionally, 'service apache2 status' checks the status of the Apache service, providing information about whether it is running or stopped. 'chkconfig' is another command-line tool for managing system services on Linux systems, primarily used on systems that use the SysV init system for service management. Users can use the 'chkconfig' command with various options to configure services to start automatically at system boot or to disable automatic startup for services.

For example, 'chkconfig sshd on' configures the SSH service to start automatically at system boot, while 'chkconfig sshd off' disables automatic startup for the SSH service, requiring manual intervention to start the service. 'chkconfig --list' displays a list of all services and their current startup statuses, allowing users to review and manage service configurations efficiently. 'systemd-analyze' is a command-line tool for analyzing the startup performance of systemd-based Linux systems. Users can use the 'systemd-analyze' command with various options to display information about system startup time, including the time taken by each service to start. For example, 'systemd-analyze blame' shows a list of services sorted by the time they took to start during system boot, helping users identify services that may be causing delays. 'systemd-analyze critical-chain' displays a graphical representation of the critical path of the system boot process, highlighting dependencies between services and identifying bottlenecks that may impact system performance. In addition to these commands, users can also use graphical tools such as 'system-config-services' or 'gnome-system-services' for managing system services on Linux systems with graphical interfaces. These tools provide user-friendly interfaces for controlling services, making it easier for users who prefer graphical interfaces to manage system services efficiently. Overall, system services are integral components of a Linux operating system, responsible for managing various aspects of system functionality, including network services, daemons, and background processes. Whether using commands such as 'systemctl', 'service', 'chkconfig', or 'systemd-analyze', users have a variety of options for managing system services effectively, ensuring system stability, reliability, and performance. Managing services with systemctl is a crucial aspect of Linux system administration, offering users a powerful and flexible toolset for controlling system services, daemons, and processes. The systemctl command is part of the systemd system and service manager, which has become the standard init system for many Linux distributions. With systemctl, users can start, stop, restart, enable, disable, reload, and check the status of services running on their systems. One of the most basic and frequently used systemctl commands is 'systemctl start', which initiates the specified service and starts it if it is not already running. For example, 'systemctl start apache2' starts the Apache HTTP Server service, enabling users to host websites and web applications. Conversely, the 'systemctl stop' command halts the specified service, terminating its execution and freeing system resources. For instance, 'systemctl stop apache2' stops the Apache service, preventing access to hosted content. 'systemctl restart' restarts the specified service, effectively stopping and then starting it again, often used to apply configuration changes or recover from issues. For example, 'systemctl restart sshd' restarts the SSH service, reloading its configuration and applying any changes made to the configuration files. Additionally, 'systemctl reload' reloads the configuration of the specified service without interrupting its execution, useful for applying configuration changes that do not require a service restart. For instance, 'systemctl reload nginx' reloads the configuration of the NGINX web server, applying any changes made to the configuration files without disrupting active connections. Another essential systemctl command is 'systemctl enable', which configures the specified service to start automatically at system boot. Enabling a service ensures that it is available as soon as the system starts up, providing continuous availability and functionality. For example, 'systemctl enable mariadb' configures the MariaDB database server to start automatically at boot, ensuring that databases are accessible immediately after the system boots.

Conversely, 'systemctl disable' deconfigures the specified service from starting automatically at system boot, requiring manual intervention to start the service. For instance, 'systemctl disable postfix' disables automatic startup for the Postfix mail transfer agent, preventing it from starting automatically when the system boots. 'systemctl status' is a command used to check the status of the specified service, providing detailed information about whether the service is running or stopped, its uptime, and any recent log entries. For example, 'systemctl status nginx' displays the current status of the NGINX web server, including whether it is running, its process ID (PID), and any recent log entries. Additionally, 'systemctl list-units' displays a list of all active units (services, sockets, devices, etc.) on the system, providing an overview of the services currently running or stopped. For example, 'systemctl list-units --type=service' displays a list of all active services on the system, along with their current status and description. 'systemctl daemon-reload' reloads the systemd manager configuration, useful after making changes to unit files or service configurations to ensure that systemd recognizes the changes. For instance, 'systemctl daemon-reload' reloads the systemd manager configuration, applying any changes made to unit files or service configurations. 'systemctl mask' is a command used to mask a service, preventing it from being started manually or automatically at system boot. Masking a service effectively disables it, making it inaccessible and preventing its execution. For example, 'systemctl mask bluetooth' masks the Bluetooth service, preventing it from starting manually or automatically at system boot. Conversely, 'systemctl unmask' reverses the masking of a service, allowing it to be started manually or automatically at system boot again. For instance, 'systemctl unmask bluetooth' unmasks the Bluetooth service, allowing it to be started manually or automatically at system boot. Overall, managing services with systemctl is an essential skill for Linux system administrators, providing a versatile and efficient way to control system services, daemons, and processes. Whether using commands such as 'start', 'stop', 'restart', 'enable', 'disable', 'reload', 'status', 'list-units', 'daemon-reload', 'mask', or 'unmask', users have a powerful toolset for managing services effectively and ensuring system stability, reliability, and performance.

Chapter 9: Basic Shell Scripting and Automation

Introduction to shell scripting is essential for Linux users and system administrators, offering a powerful way to automate repetitive tasks, streamline workflows, and enhance productivity on the command line. Shell scripting involves writing scripts or programs that are interpreted by the shell, the command-line interface used to interact with the operating system. One of the most commonly used shells for scripting on Linux systems is the Bash shell (Bourne Again SHell), which is the default shell on many distributions. To create a shell script, users can use a text editor such as 'nano' or 'vim' to write a series of commands and save them to a file with a '.sh' extension. For example, 'nano script.sh' opens the Nano text editor and creates a new file named 'script.sh', ready for writing shell commands. Once the script file has been created, users can add shell commands to perform various tasks, such as file manipulation, system administration, or data processing. Shell scripts can include basic programming constructs such as variables, loops, conditional statements, functions, and more, allowing for complex logic and decision-making within the script. For example, a simple shell script to display the current date and time can be written as follows:

bash

Copy code

```
#!/bin/bash # This is a simple shell script to display the current date and time echo "The current date and time is: $(date)"
```

In this script, the first line '#!/bin/bash' is called a shebang, which specifies the path to the shell interpreter that should be used to execute the script. The 'echo' command is used to print the specified message to the terminal, and the '$(date)' command substitution is used to insert the output of the 'date' command, which displays the current date and time. After creating a shell script file, users must make it executable using the 'chmod' command to allow it to be executed as a program. For example, 'chmod +x script.sh' makes the 'script.sh' file executable. Once the script has been made executable, users can run it like any other command by specifying its path. For example, './script.sh' executes the 'script.sh' file located in the current directory. Additionally, users can place shell scripts in directories that are included in the system PATH variable, allowing them to be executed from any directory without specifying the full path. To do this, users can move the script file to one of the directories listed in the PATH variable, such as '/usr/local/bin' or '~/bin'. For example, 'mv script.sh /usr/local/bin' moves the 'script.sh' file to the '/usr/local/bin' directory, making it accessible from anywhere on the system. Shell scripting is not only useful for automating repetitive tasks but also for creating custom solutions tailored to specific requirements. Users can leverage shell scripting to perform tasks such as system administration, log file analysis, data processing, backup and restore operations, and more. By combining shell commands, utilities, and programming constructs, users can create sophisticated scripts that automate complex workflows and improve efficiency. For example, a shell script to back up user files to a specified directory can be written as follows:

bash

Copy code

```
#!/bin/bash # This is a shell script to back up user files to a specified directory
backup_dir="/path/to/backup"
source_dir="/path/to/source"
backup_file="backup_$(date +%Y%m%d).tar.gz" # Create the backup directory if it does not exist mkdir -p "$backup_dir" # Create a compressed archive of the source directory and save it to the
```

backup directory tar -czf "$backup_dir/$backup_file" "$source_dir" echo "Backup completed successfully: $backup_dir/$backup_file"

In this script, variables are used to specify the paths to the backup directory ('backup_dir') and the source directory ('source_dir'), as well as the name of the backup file ('backup_file'). The 'mkdir -p' command creates the backup directory if it does not already exist, and the 'tar' command creates a compressed archive of the source directory and saves it to the backup directory with the specified filename. The 'date' command is used with the '%Y%m%d' format specifier to include the current date in the backup filename, ensuring that each backup has a unique name based on the date it was created. After the backup is completed, a message is printed to the terminal indicating the success of the operation. In addition to creating custom shell scripts, users can also make use of existing shell scripts and utilities available on their systems or from third-party sources. Many Linux distributions come with a wide range of pre-installed shell scripts and utilities that can be used for various purposes, such as system maintenance, package management, network administration, and more. Users can also download shell scripts and utilities from the internet or package repositories to extend the functionality of their systems further. However, it is essential to exercise caution when downloading and using shell scripts from external sources to ensure they are safe and trustworthy. Shell scripting is a valuable skill for Linux users and system administrators, offering a versatile and efficient way to automate tasks, enhance productivity, and customize system behavior. By mastering shell scripting techniques and best practices, users can unlock the full potential of the command line and leverage the power of automation to streamline their workflows and achieve their objectives more effectively. Whether creating custom scripts, using existing utilities, or collaborating with the Linux community, shell scripting opens up endless possibilities for optimizing Linux systems and maximizing their utility and efficiency.

Writing basic shell scripts for automation is a fundamental skill for Linux users and system administrators, providing a way to automate repetitive tasks, streamline workflows, and improve productivity on the command line. Shell scripting involves creating scripts or programs that are interpreted by the shell, the command-line interface used to interact with the operating system. The Bash shell (Bourne Again SHell) is one of the most commonly used shells for scripting on Linux systems and is the default shell on many distributions. To begin writing a basic shell script, users need a text editor such as 'nano' or 'vim' to write a series of commands and save them to a file with a '.sh' extension, indicating that it is a shell script. For instance, to create a simple script that prints a message to the terminal, users can open a text editor and enter the following commands:

bash

Copy code

#!/bin/bash # This is a basic shell script that prints a message to the terminal echo "Hello, world!"

In this script, the first line '#!/bin/bash' is called a shebang, which specifies the path to the shell interpreter that should be used to execute the script. The '#' character at the beginning of the second line indicates a comment, providing a description or documentation for the script. The 'echo' command is used to print the specified message 'Hello, world!' to the terminal. After creating the shell script file, users must make it executable using the 'chmod' command to allow it to be executed as a program. For example, 'chmod +x script.sh' makes the 'script.sh' file executable. Once the script has been made executable, users can run it like any other command by specifying its path. For instance, './script.sh' executes the 'script.sh' file located in the current directory. Additionally, users can place shell scripts in directories that are included in the system PATH variable, allowing them to be executed from any directory without specifying the full path. To do this, users can move the script file to one of the directories listed in the PATH variable, such as '/usr/local/bin' or '~/bin'. For instance, 'mv script.sh /usr/local/bin' moves the 'script.sh' file to the '/usr/local/bin' directory, making it accessible from anywhere on the system. Writing basic shell scripts involves using variables, loops, conditional statements, functions, and other programming constructs to perform various tasks. For example, variables can be used to store and manipulate data within a script, making it easier to manage and customize the script's behavior. To declare a variable in a shell script, users can use the following syntax:

bash

Copy code

```
#!/bin/bash # This is a basic shell script that demonstrates variable usage message="Hello, world!" echo "$message"
```

In this script, the variable 'message' is assigned the value 'Hello, world!' using the syntax 'message="Hello, world!"'. The value of the variable is then printed to the terminal using the 'echo' command. Variables in shell scripts can store various types of data, including strings, integers, arrays, and more, allowing for flexible and dynamic script behavior. Loops are another essential programming construct used in shell scripting to iterate over lists of items or perform repetitive tasks. The 'for' loop is commonly used to iterate over a list of items and perform a set of commands for each item in the list. For example, the following script uses a 'for' loop to iterate over a list of filenames and print each filename to the terminal:

bash

Copy code

```
#!/bin/bash # This is a basic shell script that demonstrates a for loop for file in *.txt; do echo "File: $file" done
```

In this script, the 'for' loop iterates over all files with a '.txt' extension in the current directory using the wildcard '*.txt'. For each file in the list, the 'echo' command prints the filename to the terminal. Conditional statements are used in shell scripting to execute different sets of commands based on specified conditions. The 'if' statement is commonly used to evaluate a condition and execute a block of commands if the condition is true. For example, the following script checks if a file exists and prints a message depending on the result:

bash

Copy code

```
#!/bin/bash # This is a basic shell script that demonstrates an if statement if [ -f "file.txt" ]; then echo "File exists: file.txt" else echo "File does not exist: file.txt" fi
```

In this script, the 'if' statement checks if the file 'file.txt' exists using the '-f' file test operator. If the file exists, the 'echo' command prints the message "File exists: file.txt" to the terminal. Otherwise, if the file does not exist, the 'echo' command prints the message "File does not exist: file.txt".

Chapter 10: Introduction to System Monitoring and Logging

Monitoring system performance is a critical aspect of Linux administration, ensuring optimal operation and identifying potential issues before they impact the system. Two commonly used command-line tools for monitoring system performance are 'top' and 'vmstat', providing real-time insights into CPU, memory, and disk usage. The 'top' command displays a dynamic overview of system processes, CPU usage, memory utilization, and other system metrics. When invoked, 'top' presents an interactive interface showing a list of processes sorted by various criteria, such as CPU usage, memory usage, and process ID. To launch 'top', simply type the command 'top' in the terminal and press Enter. Upon execution, 'top' displays a continuously updating list of processes, with details such as process ID, user, CPU usage, memory usage, and more. Users can press keys like 'M' to sort processes by memory usage, 'P' to sort by CPU usage, and 'q' to quit 'top'. Furthermore, 'top' offers options to customize its behavior, such as specifying the update interval and highlighting processes that consume the most CPU or memory. For example, 'top -d 5' refreshes the display every 5 seconds, providing near real-time updates on system performance. Another valuable command-line tool for monitoring system performance is 'vmstat', which reports virtual memory statistics, including information about system processes, memory, swap, I/O, and CPU usage. To use 'vmstat', simply type the command 'vmstat' followed by any desired options in the terminal and press Enter. By default, 'vmstat' displays a summary of system-wide statistics since the system was booted. This includes data such as the number of processes running, the amount of free memory, the amount of swap space used, and CPU utilization. Additionally, 'vmstat' provides information about system I/O activity, such as the number of blocks read and written per second. Users can specify options to customize 'vmstat's behavior, such as setting the update interval and the number of iterations. For example, 'vmstat 5 10' displays system statistics every 5 seconds for a total of 10 iterations. This provides a more granular view of system performance over a specific time period. 'top' and 'vmstat' complement each other well, offering different perspectives on system performance. While 'top' focuses on displaying real-time information about individual processes, CPU, and memory usage, 'vmstat' provides a broader overview of system-wide statistics, including memory, swap, I/O, and CPU utilization. Together, these tools enable administrators to monitor system performance effectively, identify bottlenecks, and troubleshoot issues as they arise. By regularly monitoring system performance with 'top' and 'vmstat', administrators can ensure that their systems operate efficiently and reliably, minimizing downtime and maximizing productivity. Moreover, they can proactively address performance issues before they escalate, leading to a more stable and responsive computing environment. In addition to their use in real-time monitoring, 'top' and 'vmstat' can also be incorporated into automated monitoring systems or scripts to provide continuous oversight of system performance. This allows administrators to receive alerts or take action based on predefined thresholds or conditions, ensuring proactive management of system resources and performance. Overall, 'top' and 'vmstat' are invaluable tools for Linux administrators, offering essential insights into system performance and enabling effective management of system resources. Whether used individually or in conjunction with other monitoring tools, 'top' and 'vmstat' are indispensable for maintaining system health and optimizing performance in Linux environments.

BOOK 2

RHCSA EXAM PASS

ADVANCED SYSTEM CONFIGURATION AND MANAGEMENT

ROB BOTWRIGHT

Chapter 1: Advanced File System Management and Disk Usage Optimization

Understanding system logs and log files is essential for Linux administrators, providing valuable insights into system activity, errors, and performance metrics. System logs record events and messages generated by various system components, including the kernel, services, applications, and user activities. The information stored in log files helps administrators diagnose issues, track system performance, and troubleshoot problems effectively. One of the primary locations for system logs on Linux systems is the '/var/log' directory, which contains a variety of log files organized by system component or service. To view the contents of the '/var/log' directory, administrators can use the 'ls' command, which lists the files and directories in the specified location. For example, 'ls /var/log' displays a list of log files and directories in the '/var/log' directory. Each log file in the '/var/log' directory serves a specific purpose and contains relevant information related to system activity. For instance, the 'syslog' file contains messages from the system logger daemon, which captures events from various system components and services. Administrators can use the 'cat' command to view the contents of a log file directly in the terminal. For example, 'cat /var/log/syslog' displays the contents of the 'syslog' file, allowing administrators to inspect system messages and events. Additionally, log files are typically rotated and archived periodically to prevent them from growing too large and consuming excessive disk space. Log rotation is managed by utilities such as 'logrotate', which automatically compresses and archives old log files while keeping a specified number of rotated logs for historical reference. To configure log rotation for a specific log file, administrators can create a configuration file in the '/etc/logrotate.d' directory, specifying options such as log file location, rotation frequency, compression method, and retention policy. For example, creating a configuration file named 'myapp' in the '/etc/logrotate.d' directory allows administrators to define rotation settings for the 'myapp.log' file. System logs contain various types of messages, including informational messages, warnings, errors, and critical alerts. Each message is assigned a severity level, ranging from 'debug' (least severe) to 'emergency' (most severe), allowing administrators to prioritize and address issues accordingly. To filter and view log messages based on their severity level, administrators can use utilities such as 'grep' or 'awk' to search for specific patterns or keywords within log files. For example, 'grep "error" /var/log/syslog' displays lines containing the word "error" in the 'syslog' file, helping administrators identify error messages quickly. Furthermore, administrators can configure the system logger daemon to send log messages to remote syslog servers for centralized logging and analysis. By forwarding log messages to a central server, administrators can aggregate logs from multiple systems, perform real-time monitoring and analysis, and maintain a centralized repository for auditing and compliance purposes. To configure remote logging, administrators can edit the '/etc/rsyslog.conf' file to specify the remote syslog server's address and port. For example, adding a line like '. @syslog-server:514' to the configuration file directs the system logger daemon to send all log messages to the specified syslog server. In addition to system logs, applications and services often generate their log files to record specific events and activities. These application-specific log files are typically located in directories associated with the respective applications or services. For example, web servers such as Apache or Nginx maintain access logs and error logs in directories like '/var/log/apache2' or '/var/log/nginx', respectively. Similarly, database servers like MySQL or PostgreSQL log database-related events in directories like '/var/log/mysql' or '/var/log/postgresql'. Administrators can use these application-specific log files to monitor the performance, diagnose issues, and troubleshoot errors related to specific applications or services. In summary, understanding system logs and log files is essential for Linux administrators to effectively monitor system activity, diagnose issues, and maintain system performance and reliability. By familiarizing themselves with the locations and contents of log files, administrators can leverage the information stored in logs to identify and address problems promptly, ensuring the smooth operation of Linux systems in various environments and scenarios. Additionally, administrators can employ log management best practices such as log rotation, severity-based filtering, remote logging, and application-specific logging to streamline log management processes and enhance overall system visibility and maintainability.

Disk partitioning strategies play a crucial role in organizing and managing storage resources on

Linux systems, enabling efficient use of disk space, improving performance, and enhancing data security. A disk partition is a distinct section of a physical disk drive that functions as a separate storage unit, allowing users to allocate storage space for different purposes, such as operating system installation, data storage, and system backups. Various disk partitioning schemes exist, each tailored to specific requirements and usage scenarios. One commonly used partitioning strategy is the Master Boot Record (MBR) partitioning scheme, which has been widely adopted for compatibility with legacy systems and older versions of Windows operating systems. MBR partitions are defined by partition tables stored in the disk's first sector, known as the Master Boot Record, and support up to four primary partitions or three primary partitions and one extended partition containing multiple logical partitions. To create MBR partitions on a disk, users can utilize utilities such as 'fdisk' or 'parted' to interactively define partition layouts and allocate disk space for each partition. For instance, running the command 'fdisk /dev/sda' opens the 'fdisk' utility for the disk '/dev/sda', allowing users to create, delete, and modify partitions as needed. Conversely, the GUID Partition Table (GPT) partitioning scheme has become increasingly popular due to its support for larger disk sizes, more partitions, and improved data integrity features. GPT partitions are defined by GUID partition entries stored in the disk's GUID partition table, allowing for up to 128 primary partitions per disk and eliminating the need for extended partitions and logical partitions. To create GPT partitions on a disk, users can utilize utilities such as 'gdisk' or 'parted' to interactively define partition layouts and allocate disk space for each partition. For instance, running the command 'gdisk /dev/sda' opens the 'gdisk' utility for the disk '/dev/sda', enabling users to create and manage GPT partitions. Another consideration when partitioning disks is selecting the appropriate filesystem type for each partition, which dictates how data is stored, accessed, and managed on the partition. Common filesystem types used in Linux environments include ext4, XFS, Btrfs, and NTFS (for compatibility with Windows systems). Each filesystem type offers different features, performance characteristics, and compatibility considerations, making it essential to choose the filesystem type that best suits the intended use case and requirements of each partition. To format a partition with a specific filesystem type, users can utilize utilities such as 'mkfs.ext4', 'mkfs.xfs', or 'mkfs.btrfs' to create the filesystem on the partition. For example, running the command 'mkfs.ext4 /dev/sda1' formats the partition '/dev/sda1' with the ext4 filesystem. When partitioning disks, administrators should also consider factors such as disk space allocation, partition alignment, and redundancy to optimize disk performance and ensure data reliability. Proper disk space allocation involves distributing available disk space among partitions based on their respective usage requirements, ensuring that each partition has adequate space for its intended purpose. Partition alignment refers to aligning partition boundaries with the underlying physical disk's block size, which can improve disk performance by reducing read and write overhead. Redundancy strategies such as RAID (Redundant Array of Independent Disks) can be used to enhance data reliability and availability by mirroring or striping data across multiple disks, providing fault tolerance in case of disk failures. To implement RAID configurations, users can utilize utilities such as 'mdadm' or 'fstrim' to create and manage RAID arrays with different levels of redundancy, such as RAID 0, RAID 1, RAID 5, and RAID 10. Additionally, administrators should consider the future scalability and flexibility of their partitioning scheme, allowing for easy expansion or modification of partitions as storage requirements evolve over time. This can be achieved by reserving unallocated space on the disk or using dynamic disk management features such as Logical Volume Management (LVM), which allows for flexible allocation and resizing of logical volumes across multiple physical disks. To implement LVM, users can utilize utilities such as 'pvcreate', 'vgcreate', and 'lvcreate' to create physical volumes, volume groups, and logical volumes, respectively. Overall, disk partitioning strategies are essential for organizing and managing storage resources effectively on Linux systems, enabling administrators to optimize disk performance, enhance data security, and adapt to changing storage requirements. By carefully considering factors such as partitioning schemes, filesystem types, disk space allocation, and redundancy options, administrators can create robust partitioning schemes that meet the needs of their specific use cases while allowing for future scalability and flexibility.

Chapter 2: Managing Software Repositories and Package Dependencies

File system optimization techniques are essential for improving performance, maximizing storage efficiency, and enhancing data integrity on Linux systems, ensuring optimal utilization of storage resources and maintaining system reliability. One fundamental optimization technique is choosing the appropriate filesystem type for the specific use case and requirements of the system. Linux offers a variety of filesystem types, each with its own features, performance characteristics, and suitability for different applications. Common filesystem types used in Linux environments include ext4, XFS, Btrfs, and ZFS, each offering unique advantages and considerations. To select the optimal filesystem type, administrators should evaluate factors such as performance, scalability, data integrity, and compatibility with existing systems and applications. For example, the ext4 filesystem is a widely used and mature filesystem that provides good performance and reliability for general-purpose use cases. To create an ext4 filesystem on a disk partition, administrators can use the 'mkfs.ext4' command followed by the device name of the partition. Similarly, XFS is known for its scalability and high-performance capabilities, making it well-suited for large-scale deployments and environments with heavy I/O workloads. To create an XFS filesystem, administrators can use the 'mkfs.xfs' command followed by the device name of the partition. Btrfs is a next-generation filesystem that offers advanced features such as snapshots, compression, and data deduplication, making it ideal for use cases that require flexible data management and advanced storage capabilities. To create a Btrfs filesystem, administrators can use the 'mkfs.btrfs' command followed by the device name of the partition. ZFS is a powerful filesystem and volume manager that provides features such as data integrity, snapshots, and RAID-like functionality, making it suitable for enterprise storage solutions and environments that require maximum data protection and scalability. To create a ZFS filesystem, administrators can use the 'zpool create' command followed by the name of the storage pool and the devices to be included in the pool. In addition to selecting the appropriate filesystem type, administrators can optimize file system performance by tuning various parameters and options specific to the chosen filesystem. For example, administrators can adjust parameters such as block size, inode size, journaling mode, and mount options to optimize performance, reliability, and compatibility with specific workloads and storage devices. To tune filesystem parameters, administrators can use utilities such as 'tune2fs' for ext4 filesystems, 'xfs_admin' for XFS filesystems, 'btrfs filesystem' for Btrfs filesystems, and 'zfs set' for ZFS filesystems. Another important file system optimization technique is disk partition alignment, which involves aligning partition boundaries with the underlying physical disk's block size to optimize disk I/O performance and minimize overhead. Misaligned partitions can result in suboptimal disk performance and increased wear on storage devices, especially with modern storage technologies such as solid-state drives (SSDs) and RAID arrays. To align disk partitions, administrators can use partitioning tools such as 'fdisk', 'gdisk', or 'parted' to create partitions aligned to the optimal sector size for the underlying storage device. Additionally, administrators can employ techniques such as using 4KB sector size for modern storage devices and aligning partitions to multiples of the device's physical block size for optimal performance. Furthermore, administrators can improve file system performance and efficiency by employing disk quotas and file system quotas to limit disk space usage and prevent individual users or groups from consuming excessive storage resources. Disk quotas allow administrators to set limits on the amount of disk space that users or groups can use, while file system quotas enable administrators to set limits on the number of files or inodes that users or groups can create. To enable disk quotas, administrators can use utilities such as 'quotacheck', 'quotaon', and 'edquota' to configure disk quotas for specific filesystems and users. Similarly, to enable file system quotas, administrators can use utilities such as 'setquota' and 'edquota' to configure file system quotas for specific filesystems and users. Additionally, administrators can improve file system performance and reliability by regularly monitoring and maintaining filesystems using utilities such as 'fsck' (filesystem check) and 'fstrim' (filesystem trim). Fsck is used to check and repair filesystem inconsistencies, while fstrim is used to discard unused blocks on SSDs, improving performance and prolonging the lifespan of SSDs. By incorporating these file system optimization techniques into their storage management practices, administrators can ensure optimal performance, reliability, and efficiency of file systems on Linux systems, supporting the needs of diverse workloads and applications while maximizing the value of storage resources. Repository configuration and management are integral aspects of package management on Linux systems, enabling administrators to install, update, and remove software packages from centralized repositories efficiently and securely. A software repository, often referred to as a repo, is a collection of software packages and metadata hosted on a remote server, accessible via the Internet or local network. Linux distributions typically provide default repositories containing a curated selection of software packages maintained by the distribution's developers and community. However, administrators can also configure additional repositories to access a broader range of software packages or proprietary software not included in the default repositories. One of the most common package management tools used for repository configuration and management on Linux systems is 'apt' (Advanced Package Tool), which is used in Debian-based distributions such as Ubuntu and Debian itself. To configure repositories using 'apt', administrators can edit the '/etc/apt/sources.list' file to add repository URLs and enable specific software sources. Additionally, administrators can use the 'add-apt-repository' command to add repositories easily. For example, 'add-apt-repository universe' adds the 'universe' repository to the system's software sources. Another widely used package management tool is 'yum' (Yellowdog Updater Modified), which is used in Red Hat-based distributions such as CentOS, Fedora, and Red Hat Enterprise Linux (RHEL). To configure repositories using 'yum', administrators can edit the '/etc/yum.repos.d' directory to create repository configuration files with the '.repo' extension. Additionally, administrators can use the 'yum-config-manager' command to enable or disable repositories and manage repository settings. For example, 'yum-config-manager --enable repository' enables the specified repository, while 'yum-config-manager --disable repository' disables it. In addition to 'apt' and 'yum', some distributions use other package management tools such as 'zypper' (used in openSUSE) and 'dnf' (the successor to 'yum', used in newer versions of Fedora and RHEL). These tools provide similar functionality for repository configuration and management, allowing administrators to add, enable, disable, and prioritize repositories as needed. Once repositories are configured, administrators can use package management tools to search for, install, update, and remove software packages from the enabled repositories. For example, to search for a package named 'nginx' using 'apt', administrators can run the command 'apt search nginx'. Similarly, to install the 'nginx' package, administrators can run 'apt install nginx'. To update all installed packages on the system, administrators can run 'apt update' followed by 'apt upgrade'. Similarly, with 'yum', administrators can search for packages using 'yum search nginx', install packages using 'yum install nginx', and update packages using 'yum update'. Furthermore, administrators can prioritize repositories by adjusting their repository configuration files to specify the order in which repositories are consulted when installing or updating packages. This allows administrators to control which repositories take precedence in providing package versions and dependencies. Additionally, administrators should regularly update repository metadata to ensure that package information is up-to-date and accurate. This can be done using the 'apt update' command for 'apt', the 'yum makecache' command for 'yum', or similar commands for other package management tools. By keeping repository metadata current, administrators can ensure that package installations and updates proceed smoothly without encountering errors due to outdated or missing package information. Moreover, administrators should exercise caution when adding third-party repositories or enabling additional software sources, as this can introduce security risks and compatibility issues. It is essential to verify the authenticity and trustworthiness of repositories and packages obtained from external sources to prevent the installation of malicious or compromised software. Additionally, administrators should periodically review repository configurations and remove unnecessary or obsolete repositories to reduce the risk of potential security vulnerabilities and conflicts. Overall, effective repository configuration and management are essential for maintaining system integrity, security, and reliability on Linux systems. By properly configuring repositories, updating repository metadata, and using package management tools responsibly, administrators can ensure that software installations and updates proceed smoothly and securely, supporting the needs of users and applications while minimizing the risk of security breaches and system instability.

Chapter 3: Advanced User and Group Configuration

User and group management are fundamental aspects of system administration on Linux systems, crucial for maintaining security, access control, and resource management. Proper user and group management practices help administrators organize users and assign appropriate permissions and privileges, ensuring the integrity and confidentiality of system resources. One essential best practice in user management is to adhere to the principle of least privilege, which dictates granting users only the minimum permissions required to perform their tasks effectively. By limiting users' access to only the resources and commands they need, administrators can mitigate the risk of unauthorized access and minimize the potential impact of security breaches or malicious activities. To create a new user account on a Linux system, administrators can use the 'useradd' command followed by the desired username. For example, 'useradd john' creates a new user account named 'john'. Additionally, administrators can set user account properties such as the user's home directory, default shell, and primary group using command options. For example, 'useradd -m -s /bin/bash john' creates a new user account with a home directory and sets the default shell to '/bin/bash'. Another best practice in user management is to implement strong password policies to enforce password complexity and expiration rules, reducing the risk of password-related security breaches. Administrators can configure password policies using utilities such as 'passwd' or by editing the '/etc/login.defs' file to specify parameters such as minimum password length, complexity requirements, and password expiration intervals. For example, 'passwd --maxdays 90 john' sets the maximum password age for the user 'john' to 90 days. Additionally, administrators can enforce password complexity requirements by editing the '/etc/pam.d/common-password' file and adding or modifying password-related directives. One critical aspect of user management is managing user accounts throughout their lifecycle, including provisioning, deprovisioning, and periodic review. Administrators should regularly review user accounts to identify inactive or obsolete accounts and remove them promptly to reduce the attack surface and maintain a clean and organized user database. To list all user accounts on a Linux system, administrators can use the 'cat /etc/passwd' command, which displays a list of user account information stored in the '/etc/passwd' file. Additionally, administrators can use the 'userdel' command to delete user accounts, along with the '-r' option to remove the user's home directory and files associated with the user account. For example, 'userdel -r john' deletes the user account 'john' and removes the associated home directory and files. Group management is another essential aspect of user administration, enabling administrators to organize users into logical groups and assign permissions and privileges collectively. Administrators can create new groups using the 'groupadd' command followed by the desired group name. For example, 'groupadd developers' creates a new group named 'developers'. Once groups are created, administrators can add users to groups using the 'usermod' command with the '-aG' option, followed by the group name and username. For example, 'usermod -aG developers john' adds the user 'john' to the 'developers' group. Administrators should follow naming conventions and establish a consistent group hierarchy to facilitate user management and access control. Additionally, administrators can assign group ownership to files and directories using the 'chown' command to grant group members access to shared resources. For example, 'chown :developers /var/www/html' changes the group ownership of the '/var/www/html' directory to the 'developers' group. Furthermore, administrators can manage group memberships and permissions using access control lists (ACLs), which allow for more granular control over file and directory permissions beyond traditional UNIX permissions. ACLs enable administrators to define permissions for specific users or groups on a per-file or per-directory basis, providing greater flexibility in access control. To view and modify ACLs on files and directories, administrators can use commands such as 'getfacl' and 'setfacl'. For example, 'getfacl /var/www/html' displays the ACLs set on the '/var/www/html' directory, while 'setfacl -m u:john:rwx /var/www/html/file.txt' grants the user 'john' read, write, and execute permissions on the file 'file.txt' within the '/var/www/html' directory. Regular auditing and monitoring of user and group configurations are essential to ensure compliance with security policies and detect potential security risks or policy violations. Administrators should periodically review user account settings, group memberships, and permission assignments to identify and address any discrepancies or anomalies. Additionally, administrators can leverage audit logging mechanisms to track user login activity, privilege escalation attempts, and unauthorized access attempts, providing valuable insights into system security and compliance. By following user and group management best practices, administrators can maintain a secure and well-organized user environment, effectively control access to system resources, and mitigate the risk of security breaches or unauthorized access. Implementing user and group quotas is crucial for managing disk space usage and enforcing storage limits on Linux systems, ensuring fair resource allocation and preventing individual users or groups from monopolizing available storage resources. Quotas allow administrators to define maximum disk space usage for users and groups, helping to maintain system stability, optimize disk performance, and prevent disk space exhaustion. One of the primary reasons for implementing user and group quotas is to prevent users from consuming excessive disk space, which can lead to system slowdowns, performance degradation, and potential service interruptions. By setting quotas, administrators can allocate disk space fairly among users and groups, preventing one user from adversely impacting the experience of others. To implement user and group quotas on Linux systems, administrators can use the quota management utilities provided by the operating system, such as 'quota' and 'edquota'. These utilities allow administrators to set, modify, and monitor disk quotas for individual users and groups, providing granular control over disk space usage. Before enabling quotas, administrators must first ensure that the quota management tools are installed on the system. On many Linux distributions, these tools are included by default, but they can also be installed using the distribution's package manager if necessary. Once installed, administrators can enable quotas on specific filesystems by adding the 'usrquota' and 'grpquota' options to the filesystem's entry in the '/etc/fstab' file. For example, modifying the entry for the '/home' filesystem in the '/etc/fstab' file to include the 'usrquota' and 'grpquota' options enables user and group quotas on the '/home' directory. After enabling quotas, administrators can set quotas for individual users and groups using the 'edquota' command. This command opens a text editor where administrators can specify the soft and hard limits for disk space usage for each user or group. Soft limits define the maximum amount of disk space a user or group can use before receiving warnings, while hard limits define the absolute maximum disk space allowed, enforcing strict quotas. For example, running the command 'edquota -u john' opens the quota editor for the user 'john', allowing administrators to set disk space limits for the user. Similarly, running the command 'edquota -g developers' opens the quota editor for the 'developers' group, enabling administrators to set disk space limits for the group. Administrators can also view the current disk space usage and quota status for users and groups using the 'quota' command. This command displays a summary of disk space usage, soft and hard limits, and quota enforcement status for each user and group with quotas enabled. For example, running the command 'quota -u john' displays quota information for the user 'john', while 'quota -g developers' displays quota information for the 'developers' group. In addition to setting and monitoring quotas, administrators can configure email notifications to alert users when they approach or exceed their disk space quotas. This helps users proactively manage their disk space usage and avoid potential quota violations. Administrators can configure email notifications by editing the '/etc/aliases' file to specify the email addresses of users who should receive quota notifications. For example, adding a line such as 'john: john@example.com' to the '/etc/aliases' file directs quota notifications for the user 'john' to the email address 'john@example.com'. After editing the '/etc/aliases' file, administrators must run the 'newaliases' command to update the email alias database and apply the changes. Once email notifications are configured, users will receive automatic notifications when they approach or exceed their disk space quotas, allowing them to take corrective action as needed. Overall, implementing user and group quotas is an essential practice for managing disk space usage on Linux systems, ensuring fair resource allocation, and preventing disk space-related issues. By setting and enforcing quotas, administrators can optimize disk usage, maintain system stability, and promote efficient resource utilization across users and groups.

Chapter 4: Securing File Systems with Access Control Lists (ACLs)

Understanding access control lists (ACLs) is crucial for implementing fine-grained access control and managing permissions on Linux systems, providing a flexible and granular way to define access rights for users and groups beyond traditional UNIX permissions. An ACL is a set of rules associated with a file or directory that specifies which users or groups have permissions to perform specific actions, such as reading, writing, or executing files, and allows administrators to define access permissions for multiple users and groups simultaneously. ACLs extend the basic read, write, and execute permissions provided by traditional UNIX file permissions, enabling administrators to grant or restrict access to files and directories based on more complex criteria, such as user identity, group membership, or specific permissions. To view the ACLs set on a file or directory, administrators can use the 'getfacl' command followed by the path to the file or directory. This command displays the ACL entries associated with the specified file or directory, including the permissions granted to users and groups, as well as any default ACL entries inherited from parent directories. For example, running 'getfacl /path/to/file' displays the ACL entries for the file located at '/path/to/file'. In addition to viewing ACLs, administrators can set and modify ACLs using the 'setfacl' command. This command allows administrators to add, modify, or remove ACL entries for files and directories, granting or revoking specific permissions for users and groups as needed. For example, to grant read and write permissions to a specific user on a file, administrators can use the command 'setfacl -m u:username:rw /path/to/file', where 'username' is the name of the user and '/path/to/file' is the path to the file. Similarly, to grant read and execute permissions to a specific group on a directory and all its contents recursively, administrators can use the command 'setfacl -R -m g:groupname:rx /path/to/directory'. ACL entries consist of three components: the type of entry (user, group, or other), the identity to which the entry applies (username, groupname, or 'other'), and the permissions granted or revoked (read, write, execute, or a combination thereof). Additionally, ACLs may include default entries that specify the default permissions applied to newly created files and directories within the parent directory. Default ACL entries allow administrators to define a consistent set of permissions for all files and directories created within a specific directory, ensuring uniform access control across the filesystem hierarchy. To set default ACL entries on a directory, administrators can use the 'setfacl' command with the '-d' option, followed by the desired ACL entries. For example, 'setfacl -d -m u::rwx,g::r-x,o::--- /path/to/directory' sets default ACL entries on the directory '/path/to/directory' to grant read, write, and execute permissions to the owner, read and execute permissions to the group, and no permissions to others. ACLs offer several advantages over traditional UNIX permissions, including the ability to grant permissions to specific users and groups without affecting others, support for more fine-grained access control, and the ability to set default permissions for newly created files and directories. However, it is essential to use ACLs judiciously and understand their implications, as overly complex ACL configurations can lead to confusion, security vulnerabilities, and unintended consequences. Administrators should carefully plan ACL configurations, regularly audit ACL settings, and document ACL usage to ensure consistency, security, and compliance with organizational policies and regulatory requirements.

Additionally, administrators should be aware of the interaction between ACLs and traditional UNIX permissions, as conflicts or inconsistencies between ACLs and permissions can lead to unexpected behavior and security risks. Overall, understanding ACLs is essential for effective access control and permission management on Linux systems, enabling administrators to implement flexible and robust security policies that meet the needs of users and applications while maintaining the integrity and confidentiality of system resources.

Implementing ACLs for enhanced file security is a crucial aspect of managing access control on Linux systems, providing administrators with a powerful tool to enforce fine-grained permissions and restrict access to sensitive files and directories. ACLs extend the traditional UNIX permissions model by allowing administrators to define access permissions for specific users and groups beyond the owner, group, and other categories. This enables administrators to grant or revoke permissions selectively, based on user identity, group membership, or other criteria, ensuring that only authorized users can access or modify protected files and directories. To begin implementing ACLs, administrators must first ensure that the filesystem supports ACLs and that ACL functionality is enabled. Most modern Linux filesystems, such as ext4 and XFS, support ACLs by default, but administrators can verify ACL support using the 'mount' command with the '-l' option to display filesystem mount options. For example, running 'mount -l | grep acl' checks if ACL support is enabled for all mounted filesystems. Once ACL support is confirmed, administrators can set ACLs on files and directories using the 'setfacl' command. This command allows administrators to add, modify, or remove ACL entries to define access permissions for users and groups. For example, 'setfacl -m u:username:rw /path/to/file' grants read and write permissions to the user specified by 'username' on the file located at '/path/to/file'. Similarly, 'setfacl -m g:groupname:r /path/to/directory' grants read permissions to the group specified by 'groupname' on the directory '/path/to/directory'. In addition to setting ACLs manually, administrators can also use default ACLs to apply consistent permissions to all files and directories created within a specific directory. Default ACLs allow administrators to define a template of permissions that are automatically applied to newly created files and directories, ensuring uniform access control throughout the filesystem hierarchy. To set default ACLs, administrators can use the '-d' option with the 'setfacl' command followed by the desired ACL entries. For example, 'setfacl -d -m u::rwx,g::r-x,o::- /path/to/directory' sets default ACLs on the directory '/path/to/directory' to grant read, write, and execute permissions to the owner, read and execute permissions to the group, and no permissions to others. Additionally, administrators can use the 'getfacl' command to view the ACLs set on files and directories. This command displays a detailed listing of all ACL entries associated with the specified file or directory, including the permissions granted to users and groups. For example, running 'getfacl /path/to/file' displays the ACL entries for the file located at '/path/to/file'. Regular monitoring and auditing of ACL configurations are essential to ensure that access permissions remain consistent with security policies and regulatory requirements. Administrators should periodically review ACL settings, identify any discrepancies or inconsistencies, and take corrective action as needed to maintain file security. Furthermore, administrators should document ACL configurations and ensure that all relevant stakeholders are aware of access permissions and restrictions to prevent unauthorized access or accidental data breaches. By implementing ACLs for enhanced file security, administrators can enforce fine-grained access control, protect sensitive data, and mitigate the risk of unauthorized access or data leakage, ensuring the integrity and confidentiality of system resources.

Chapter 5: Advanced Networking Configuration and Troubleshooting

Advanced network configuration tools and utilities play a vital role in managing and optimizing network connectivity on Linux systems, providing administrators with the necessary tools to configure network interfaces, troubleshoot network issues, and monitor network performance effectively. One of the most commonly used network configuration tools on Linux systems is 'ifconfig', which allows administrators to view and configure network interface parameters, such as IP addresses, netmasks, and broadcast addresses. For example, 'ifconfig eth0 192.168.1.10 netmask 255.255.255.0' assigns the IP address '192.168.1.10' and netmask '255.255.255.0' to the network interface 'eth0'. However, 'ifconfig' has been deprecated in favor of the more modern 'ip' command, which provides additional functionality and flexibility for network configuration tasks. The 'ip' command allows administrators to perform various network-related tasks, such as configuring network interfaces, routing tables, and ARP cache entries. For example, 'ip addr add

192.168.1.10/24 dev eth0' assigns the IP address '192.168.1.10' with a subnet mask of '24' to the network interface 'eth0'. Additionally, the 'ip' command can be used to manipulate routing tables and manage network routes. Administrators can add, delete, or modify routes using commands such as 'ip route add', 'ip route del', and 'ip route change'. For example, 'ip route add default via 192.168.1.1' adds a default route via the gateway '192.168.1.1' to the routing table. Another useful tool for advanced network configuration is 'netplan', a YAML-based network configuration utility introduced in modern Linux distributions, such as Ubuntu. Netplan allows administrators to define network configuration settings in a simple and structured format, making it easier to manage complex network configurations across multiple interfaces and systems. Administrators can define network interfaces, IP addresses, routes, and DNS settings in the Netplan configuration file located in '/etc/netplan/'. For example, configuring a static IP address for a network interface using Netplan involves editing the configuration file to specify the desired network configuration parameters. Additionally, administrators can use network monitoring tools to assess network performance and troubleshoot connectivity issues effectively.

One such tool is 'ping', which sends ICMP echo request packets to a specified host and measures the round-trip time for the packets to reach the destination and return. For example, 'ping 192.168.1.1' sends ICMP echo requests to the IP address '192.168.1.1' and displays the round-trip time for each packet. Another useful network monitoring tool is 'traceroute', which traces the route that packets take from the source to the destination, showing each hop along the way and the round-trip time to reach each hop. For example, 'traceroute google.com' traces the route to the host 'google.com' and displays the IP addresses and round-trip times for each hop. Additionally, administrators can use packet capture tools, such as 'tcpdump' and 'Wireshark', to capture and analyze network traffic in real-time, helping to diagnose network issues and identify potential security threats. Tcpdump captures network packets on a specified interface and displays packet headers and content in a human-readable format. For example, 'sudo tcpdump -i eth0' captures network packets on the 'eth0' interface and displays packet information in real-time. Wireshark is a graphical packet analyzer that provides a more user-friendly interface for capturing and analyzing network traffic. Administrators can use Wireshark to inspect packet headers, filter packets based on specific criteria, and analyze packet contents in detail. Overall, advanced network configuration tools and utilities are essential for managing and optimizing network connectivity on Linux systems, providing administrators with the necessary capabilities to configure network interfaces, troubleshoot network issues, and monitor network performance effectively. Troubleshooting complex networking issues is a fundamental skill for system administrators and network engineers, as it involves identifying and resolving problems that affect network connectivity, performance, and reliability. One of the first steps in troubleshooting complex networking issues is to gather information about the problem by using diagnostic tools such as 'ping', which sends ICMP echo requests to a specified host to check for network connectivity. For example, running 'ping google.com' checks if the system can reach the Google website and measures the round-trip time for packets to reach the destination and return. If the 'ping' command fails to reach the destination, it indicates a potential network connectivity issue that requires further investigation. In such cases, administrators can use the 'traceroute' command to trace the route that packets take from the source to the destination, showing each hop along the way and the round-trip time to reach each hop. For example, running 'traceroute google.com' traces the route to the Google website and displays the IP addresses and round-trip times for each hop. By analyzing the output of 'traceroute', administrators can identify network devices or routers that may be causing delays or packet loss along the path. Another useful diagnostic tool for troubleshooting complex networking issues is 'netstat', which displays network statistics and information about active network connections, routing tables, and network interfaces. For example, running 'netstat -nr' displays the routing table, showing the list of network destinations and the corresponding gateway addresses and interface names. Administrators can use 'netstat' to identify misconfigured routes, duplicate IP addresses, or network congestion issues that may affect network connectivity. In addition to diagnostic tools, administrators can use packet capture tools such as 'tcpdump' and 'Wireshark' to capture and analyze network traffic in real-time, helping to diagnose network issues and identify potential security threats. Tcpdump captures network packets on a specified interface and displays packet headers and content in a human-readable format. For example, running 'sudo tcpdump -i eth0' captures network packets on the 'eth0' interface and displays packet information in real-time. Wireshark is a graphical packet analyzer that provides a more user-friendly interface for capturing and analyzing network traffic. Administrators can use Wireshark to inspect packet headers, filter packets based on specific criteria, and analyze packet contents in detail. Additionally, administrators can use system log files to troubleshoot complex networking issues by examining log entries related to network services, interfaces, and routing protocols. Log files such as '/var/log/messages' and '/var/log/syslog' contain valuable information about network events, errors, and warnings that can help identify the root cause of networking problems. By reviewing log files, administrators can pinpoint configuration errors, software bugs, or hardware failures that may be affecting network performance. Furthermore, administrators can use network monitoring tools such as 'Nagios' and 'Zabbix' to monitor network devices, services, and performance metrics in real-time, helping to detect and alert on potential issues before they escalate into problems. These tools provide a centralized dashboard for monitoring network health, displaying status information, alerts, and performance graphs for critical network resources. By proactively monitoring network infrastructure and performance, administrators can identify and resolve issues quickly, minimizing downtime and ensuring optimal network reliability and performance. Overall, troubleshooting complex networking issues requires a combination of diagnostic tools, analytical skills, and hands-on experience to identify and resolve problems effectively. By following a systematic approach to troubleshooting and using the right tools and techniques, administrators can diagnose and resolve even the most challenging networking issues, ensuring the stability, security, and performance of their network infrastructure.

Chapter 6: Managing Services and Daemons

Advanced service management with systemd is a critical aspect of system administration on modern Linux distributions, providing administrators with powerful tools to manage and control system services, daemons, and processes efficiently. One of the key features of systemd is its unit file system, which defines how services, sockets, devices, and other system resources are managed and controlled. Unit files are configuration files that describe the properties and dependencies of a particular system unit, such as a service or a target. Administrators can use unit files to define the behavior of system services, including startup behavior, resource limits, environment variables, and dependencies on other services. Unit files are typically stored in the '/etc/systemd/system/' directory and have a '.service' extension for services, '.socket' for sockets, and '.target' for targets. To create a new service unit file, administrators can use a text editor to create a new file with the '.service' extension in the '/etc/systemd/system/' directory and define the necessary configuration settings. For example, creating a service unit file for a custom application involves specifying the executable path, command-line arguments, working directory, user, group, and any additional configuration options. Once the unit file is created, administrators can use the 'systemctl' command to manage the service, including starting, stopping, enabling, disabling, and restarting it. For example, 'systemctl start myservice.service' starts the service named 'myservice', while 'systemctl enable myservice.service' enables the service to start automatically at boot time. Additionally, administrators can use the 'systemctl status' command to view the status of a service and check if it is running, enabled, or failed. For example, 'systemctl status myservice.service' displays detailed information about the status of the 'myservice' service, including its current state, PID, and any error messages or warnings. Systemd also provides advanced features for managing service dependencies and ordering, allowing administrators to define the order in which services are started and stopped and ensure that dependencies are met before starting a service. Administrators can use directives such as 'Requires', 'Wants', 'After', and 'Before' in unit files to specify service dependencies and ordering requirements. For example, adding the line

'Wants=network-online.target' to a service unit file ensures that the service starts after the network is up and running. Systemd also supports service templating, which allows administrators to define a template unit file with placeholder variables and dynamically instantiate multiple instances of the same service with different configurations. This is particularly useful for managing multiple instances of similar services, such as web servers or database servers, with different configuration settings. Administrators can use directives such as '%i' and '%f' in unit files to specify template variables and instantiate multiple instances of a service with different instance names or file paths. For example, creating a template unit file for a web server involves defining placeholder variables for the port number and document root directory, which can be customized when instantiating the service. Systemd also provides advanced logging and journaling capabilities, allowing administrators to collect, store, and analyze log messages from system services and processes centrally. The systemd journal, stored in binary format under '/var/log/journal/', contains detailed information about system events, service start-up and shutdown, kernel messages, and user activity. Administrators can use the 'journalctl' command to query and filter journal entries based on various criteria, such as time range, priority level, service name, or specific keywords. For example, 'journalctl -u myservice.service' displays log messages related to the 'myservice' service, while 'journalctl -p err' displays only error messages. Overall, advanced service management with systemd empowers administrators to configure, manage, and troubleshoot system services effectively, providing a robust and flexible framework for managing the lifecycle of system processes and ensuring the stability and reliability of Linux systems. By leveraging systemd's features and capabilities, administrators can streamline service management tasks, optimize system performance, and maintain the integrity of critical system services in complex IT environments. Service optimization techniques are essential for enhancing the performance, reliability, and efficiency of system services on Linux systems, enabling administrators to maximize resource utilization and minimize downtime. One of the key techniques for optimizing services is to fine-tune service configuration settings to optimize resource usage and improve performance. For example, administrators can adjust parameters such as memory limits, CPU affinity, and I/O priority to ensure that services have access to adequate resources and are not competing for system resources with other processes. This can be achieved by modifying the service unit file, typically located in the '/etc/systemd/system/' directory, and adjusting the relevant configuration options using a text editor. Another important aspect of service optimization is to identify and eliminate performance bottlenecks by profiling and analyzing service performance using monitoring tools such as 'systemd-analyze' and 'systemd-cgtop'. These tools provide insights into service startup times, resource usage, and dependencies, allowing administrators to identify areas for improvement and optimize service configuration settings accordingly. Additionally, administrators can leverage caching mechanisms to improve service performance and reduce latency by storing frequently accessed data in memory or on disk. For example, configuring a caching proxy server such as 'Squid' or 'Nginx' can help accelerate web content delivery and reduce bandwidth usage by caching static content and serving it directly to clients without the need to fetch it from the origin server every time. Similarly, enabling database query caching can improve database performance by caching query results in memory and serving them to clients without executing the query again. Administrators can also optimize service performance by implementing load balancing and clustering techniques to distribute incoming requests across multiple servers or instances, ensuring high availability and scalability. Load balancing solutions such as 'HAProxy' and 'Nginx' can distribute incoming traffic to backend servers based on predefined algorithms such as round-robin, least connections, or IP hashing, ensuring optimal resource utilization and preventing overload on individual servers. Similarly, clustering solutions such as 'Pacemaker' and 'Corosync' can coordinate the operation of multiple servers to provide fault tolerance and high availability for critical services, automatically migrating services to healthy nodes in the event of a failure. Another effective technique for service optimization is to optimize database performance by tuning database configuration settings, indexing, and query optimization. For example, administrators can adjust parameters such as buffer cache size, query cache size, and thread concurrency to optimize database performance and improve responsiveness. Additionally, creating appropriate indexes on database tables can accelerate query execution by facilitating fast data retrieval and reducing the need for full table scans. Administrators can also optimize disk I/O performance by using techniques such as RAID (Redundant Array of Independent Disks) and SSD (Solid State Drive) caching to improve disk throughput and reduce latency. RAID configurations such as RAID 0 (striping) and RAID 10 (mirroring and striping) can improve disk performance by distributing data across multiple disks and enabling parallel read and write operations. Similarly, SSD caching solutions such as 'dm-cache' and 'bcache' can improve disk I/O performance by caching frequently accessed data on high-speed SSDs, reducing latency and improving overall system responsiveness. Additionally, administrators can optimize network performance by configuring network interfaces, tuning TCP/IP parameters, and optimizing network protocols to minimize packet loss, latency, and jitter. For example, adjusting parameters such as TCP window size, congestion control algorithms, and network buffer sizes can improve TCP/IP performance and throughput. Similarly, enabling jumbo frames and network offloading features such as TCP segmentation offload (TSO) and large receive offload (LRO) can reduce CPU overhead and improve network efficiency. Overall, service optimization techniques are essential for maximizing the performance, reliability, and efficiency of system services on Linux systems, enabling administrators to optimize resource usage, improve service responsiveness, and ensure high availability and scalability in complex IT environments. By leveraging a combination of configuration tuning, caching mechanisms, load balancing, clustering, database optimization, and disk and network performance tuning techniques, administrators can optimize service performance and deliver a seamless and responsive user experience for critical applications and services

Chapter 7: Implementing Remote Access and SSH Security

Secure SSH configuration practices are essential for ensuring the integrity, confidentiality, and availability of remote access to Linux systems, protecting against unauthorized access, data breaches, and malicious attacks. One of the fundamental steps in securing SSH is to disable root login and restrict access to privileged accounts to prevent attackers from gaining unauthorized access to the system. This can be achieved by modifying the SSH configuration file, typically located at '/etc/ssh/sshd_config', and setting the 'PermitRootLogin' directive to 'no' to disable root login. Additionally, administrators can create separate user accounts with limited privileges and grant sudo privileges as needed to perform administrative tasks, reducing the risk of privilege escalation attacks. Another important aspect of SSH security is to enforce strong password policies and implement multi-factor authentication (MFA) to enhance authentication security and prevent password-based attacks. Administrators can configure SSH to enforce password complexity requirements, such as minimum length, complexity, and expiration, using the 'PasswordAuthentication' and 'UsePAM' directives in the SSH configuration file. Additionally, administrators can implement MFA using tools such as 'Google Authenticator' or 'Duo Security' to require users to provide a second form of authentication, such as a one-time password (OTP) or biometric authentication, in addition to their password when logging in. This adds an extra layer of security and mitigates the risk of brute-force attacks and credential theft. Furthermore, administrators can enhance SSH security by configuring SSH key-based authentication, which uses cryptographic key pairs instead of passwords for authentication, providing a more secure and convenient method for authenticating users. To enable SSH key-based authentication, administrators can generate an SSH key pair using the 'ssh-keygen' command on the client machine and copy the public key to the remote server's '~/.ssh/authorized_keys' file. Additionally, administrators can restrict SSH access to specific IP addresses or ranges using firewall rules or TCP wrapper configurations to limit exposure to potential attackers and mitigate the risk of brute-force attacks. For example, administrators can use the 'iptables' or 'firewalld' commands to configure firewall rules to allow SSH access only from trusted IP addresses or networks, such as corporate VPNs or known administrative IP addresses. Similarly, administrators can use TCP wrappers to specify access control rules for SSH in the '/etc/hosts.allow' and '/etc/hosts.deny' files to allow or deny SSH access based on the client's IP address or hostname. Moreover, administrators can monitor and log SSH activity to detect and respond to suspicious behavior, unauthorized access attempts, and security incidents in real-time. By enabling SSH logging in the SSH configuration file and configuring syslog or auditd to capture SSH log messages, administrators can track user logins, authentication failures, and session activity, allowing them to identify potential security threats and take appropriate action to mitigate risks. Additionally, administrators can implement automated intrusion detection and prevention systems (IDS/IPS) to monitor SSH traffic for signs of malicious activity, such as repeated failed login attempts, brute-force attacks, or suspicious connection patterns, and automatically block or alert on suspicious activity. Overall, secure SSH configuration practices are essential for protecting Linux systems against unauthorized access, data breaches, and malicious attacks, ensuring the confidentiality, integrity, and availability of critical resources and sensitive information. By following best practices such as disabling root login, enforcing strong password policies, implementing multi-factor authentication, configuring SSH key-based authentication, restricting access to trusted IP addresses, monitoring and logging SSH activity, and implementing automated intrusion detection and prevention systems, administrators can strengthen SSH security and reduce the risk of security incidents and data breaches. Remote access management and security measures are crucial aspects of system administration, ensuring secure and reliable access to remote systems while mitigating the risk of unauthorized access, data breaches, and malicious attacks. One of the fundamental security measures for remote access management is to use secure protocols such as SSH (Secure Shell) or VPN (Virtual Private Network) to establish encrypted connections between remote clients and servers, protecting data confidentiality and integrity during transmission. Administrators can use the 'ssh' command to establish SSH connections to remote systems, providing encrypted communication channels for secure remote access and file transfer. Additionally, administrators can set up VPNs using tools such as

OpenVPN or IPsec to create secure, private networks over the internet, allowing remote users to access internal resources securely. Another important aspect of remote access security is to implement strong authentication mechanisms to verify the identities of remote users and devices before granting access to sensitive systems and data. This can be achieved by using multi-factor authentication (MFA) techniques such as one-time passwords (OTP), biometric authentication, or hardware tokens in combination with usernames and passwords. Administrators can configure MFA using tools such as Google Authenticator or Duo Security to require users to provide additional authentication factors beyond their passwords when logging in remotely. Additionally, administrators can enforce strong password policies, such as password complexity requirements, expiration periods, and account lockout policies, to prevent password-based attacks and enhance authentication security. Administrators can use tools like 'passwd' or 'chpasswd' to set or update user passwords and 'pam_tally2' to configure account lockout policies based on failed login attempts. Furthermore, administrators can implement access control mechanisms to restrict remote access to authorized users and devices based on predefined policies and rules. This can be achieved by configuring firewall rules, TCP wrappers, or access control lists (ACLs) to allow or deny remote connections based on source IP addresses, user identities, or authentication tokens. For example, administrators can use the 'iptables' or 'firewalld' commands to configure firewall rules to allow SSH access only from trusted IP addresses or networks. Similarly, administrators can use TCP wrappers to specify access control rules for SSH in the '/etc/hosts.allow' and '/etc/hosts.deny' files to allow or deny SSH access based on the client's IP address or hostname. Additionally, administrators can implement role-based access control (RBAC) policies to grant different levels of access privileges to remote users based on their roles, responsibilities, and job functions. RBAC allows administrators to define granular access permissions for different resources and services, ensuring that users have the minimum necessary privileges to perform their tasks without compromising security. Administrators can use tools such as 'sudo' or 'sudoers' to configure RBAC policies and define sudo rules for specific users or groups, specifying which commands they are allowed to run with elevated privileges. Moreover, administrators can monitor and audit remote access activity to detect and respond to security incidents, unauthorized access attempts, and policy violations in real-time. By enabling logging and auditing features in SSH, VPN, and authentication servers, administrators can track user logins, session activity, and authentication events, allowing them to identify potential security threats and take appropriate action to mitigate risks. Additionally, administrators can use intrusion detection and prevention systems (IDS/IPS) to monitor network traffic for signs of suspicious activity and automatically block or alert on unauthorized access attempts or security breaches. Overall, remote access management and security measures are essential for protecting sensitive systems and data from unauthorized access, data breaches, and cyber threats, ensuring the confidentiality, integrity, and availability of critical resources and services. By implementing secure protocols, strong authentication mechanisms, access control policies, RBAC, and monitoring and auditing mechanisms, administrators can establish secure remote access environments and mitigate the risk of security incidents and compliance violations.

Chapter 8: Configuring and Managing Firewalls

Introduction to firewalls and packet filtering is fundamental to understanding network security principles and safeguarding computer systems against unauthorized access and malicious activity. A firewall acts as a barrier between an internal network and external networks, such as the internet, controlling the flow of network traffic based on predefined rules and policies. One of the most common types of firewalls is a packet filtering firewall, which examines individual packets of data as they pass through the network and makes decisions about whether to allow or block them based on specified criteria. Packet filtering firewalls operate at the network layer of the OSI model, inspecting packet headers and payload contents to determine whether they meet the criteria defined in the firewall rules. Administrators can use packet filtering rules to define what types of traffic are allowed or denied based on criteria such as source and destination IP addresses, port numbers, and protocol types. For example, administrators can use the 'iptables' command on Linux systems to create packet filtering rules that allow or block traffic based on various criteria. To allow inbound SSH traffic from a specific IP address, administrators can use the command 'iptables -A INPUT -p tcp --dport 22 -s <source_ip> -j ACCEPT'. Conversely, to block inbound SSH traffic from all other IP addresses, administrators can use the command 'iptables -A INPUT -p tcp --dport 22 -j DROP'. Additionally, administrators can use packet filtering to implement stateful inspection, which tracks the state of network connections and allows only legitimate traffic that is part of an established connection to pass through the firewall. Stateful inspection firewalls maintain a state table that records information about each active connection, such as source and destination IP addresses, port numbers, and connection status. This allows the firewall to make more intelligent decisions about which packets to allow or block based on the context of the connection. For example, if a client initiates an outbound TCP connection to a remote server, the firewall will create an entry in the state table to track the connection's state. Subsequent packets belonging to the same connection will be allowed to pass through the firewall based on the state table entry, while packets that do not match any existing connection state will be dropped or rejected. In addition to filtering based on source and destination IP addresses and port numbers, administrators can use packet filtering to implement more advanced filtering criteria, such as filtering based on packet contents, packet size, and packet timing. For example, administrators can use the 'tcpdump' command to capture network traffic and analyze packet contents to identify suspicious or malicious activity. By examining packet payloads and looking for specific patterns or signatures, administrators can detect and block unauthorized access attempts, denial-of-service (DoS) attacks, and other security threats. Furthermore, administrators can use packet filtering to implement network address translation (NAT), which allows multiple internal hosts to share a single public IP address when accessing the internet. NAT modifies the source or destination IP addresses of packets as they pass through the firewall, translating private IP addresses to a single public IP address and vice versa. This helps preserve the limited supply of public IP addresses and adds an extra layer of security by hiding internal network topology from external networks. For example, administrators can use the 'iptables' command to configure NAT rules that translate internal private IP addresses to a single public IP address when accessing the internet. To configure outbound NAT for a specific internal network interface, administrators can use the command 'iptables -t nat -A POSTROUTING -o <interface> -j MASQUERADE'. Overall, introduction to firewalls and packet filtering is essential for understanding network security concepts and implementing effective security measures to protect computer systems and networks from unauthorized access, data breaches, and cyber attacks. By deploying packet filtering firewalls and configuring appropriate filtering rules, administrators can control the flow of network traffic and enforce security policies to safeguard sensitive information and ensure the integrity and availability of network resources. Advanced firewall configuration with iptables or firewalld is essential for implementing robust network security measures and protecting computer systems and networks from various cyber threats and unauthorized access attempts. Iptables and firewalld are powerful firewall management tools available on Linux systems, offering extensive capabilities for defining firewall rules, filtering network traffic, and enforcing security policies. These tools allow administrators to create sophisticated firewall configurations to control the flow of network traffic based on specific criteria such as source and destination IP addresses, port numbers, and protocol types. With iptables, administrators can create and manage firewall rules using the 'iptables' command-line utility, which provides a comprehensive set of options and parameters for defining packet filtering rules, network address translation (NAT), and connection tracking. For example, administrators can use iptables to configure stateful packet filtering rules that track the state of network connections and allow only legitimate traffic that is part of an established connection to pass through the firewall. To create a stateful firewall rule that allows incoming SSH traffic while blocking all other incoming traffic, administrators can use the following iptables command: 'iptables -A INPUT -m state --state RELATED,ESTABLISHED -j ACCEPT' followed by 'iptables -A INPUT -p tcp --dport 22 -j ACCEPT' to allow incoming SSH traffic on port 22. Conversely, administrators can use firewalld to manage firewall rules using a more user-friendly and dynamic approach, leveraging concepts such as zones, services, and rich rules to define firewall policies. Firewalld provides a higher-level abstraction of firewall management compared to iptables, allowing administrators to configure firewall rules using predefined service definitions or custom rulesets. For example, administrators can use firewalld to configure a public zone that allows inbound SSH traffic while blocking all other inbound traffic by running the following commands: 'firewall-cmd --zone=public --add-service=ssh' to allow SSH traffic and 'firewall-cmd --zone=public --remove-service=dhcpv6-client' to remove the DHCPv6-client service from the public zone. Additionally, firewalld supports the concept of dynamic firewall rules called rich rules, which allow administrators to define more complex firewall rules based on arbitrary criteria such as IP address ranges, port ranges, and packet attributes. Rich rules provide greater flexibility and granularity in firewall configuration, enabling administrators to create more sophisticated security policies tailored to their specific requirements. For example, administrators can use firewalld to define a rich rule that allows incoming SSH traffic from a specific IP address range while blocking all other incoming traffic by running the following command: 'firewall-cmd --zone=public --add-rich-rule='rule family="ipv4" source address="192.168.1.0/24" port port="22" protocol="tcp" accept'' to allow SSH traffic from the 192.168.1.0/24 subnet. Furthermore, both iptables and firewalld support the configuration of network address translation (NAT) rules, which allow administrators to modify the source or destination IP addresses of packets as they pass through the firewall. NAT is commonly used to translate internal private IP addresses to a single public IP address when accessing the internet, preserving the limited supply of public IP addresses and adding an extra layer of security by hiding internal network topology from external networks. Administrators can use iptables or firewalld to configure NAT rules by defining NAT table chains and specifying translation rules based on packet attributes such as source and destination IP addresses and port numbers. For example, administrators can use iptables to configure outbound NAT for a specific internal network interface by running the following commands: 'iptables -t nat -A POSTROUTING -o <interface> -j MASQUERADE' to enable NAT masquerading for outbound traffic on the specified interface. Overall, advanced firewall configuration with iptables or firewalld is essential for implementing robust network security measures and protecting computer systems and networks from unauthorized access attempts, data breaches, and cyber attacks. By leveraging the powerful features and capabilities of iptables and firewalld, administrators can create sophisticated firewall configurations tailored to their specific requirements and ensure the integrity, confidentiality, and availability of network resources.

Chapter 9: Implementing File Sharing and Network Services

Setting up and securing Network File Systems (NFS) is crucial for facilitating file sharing and collaboration among multiple systems in a networked environment while ensuring data integrity, confidentiality, and availability. NFS is a distributed file system protocol that allows remote systems to access shared files and directories over a network, enabling users to access and manipulate files as if they were stored locally on their own systems. Setting up NFS involves configuring both the NFS server, which hosts the shared files and directories, and the NFS clients, which access and mount the shared file systems. On Linux systems, the NFS server is typically implemented using the NFS server daemon (nfsd), while NFS clients use the mount command to mount remote file systems onto local directories. To set up an NFS server on a Linux system, administrators must first install the NFS server package, which includes the necessary utilities and configuration files for setting up and managing NFS exports. On distributions like Ubuntu or Debian, administrators can install the

NFS server package by running the command 'sudo apt-get install nfs-kernel-server', while on distributions like CentOS or Red Hat Enterprise Linux (RHEL), they can use the command 'sudo yum install nfs-utils'. Once the NFS server package is installed, administrators can configure NFS exports by editing the '/etc/exports' file, which specifies the shared directories and their access permissions for remote clients. Each line in the '/etc/exports' file represents a shared directory and its associated configuration parameters, such as the export path, allowed client IP addresses or hostnames, and access permissions. For example, to export the '/shared' directory to a specific client with IP address 192.168.1.100 with read-write access, administrators can add the following line to the '/etc/exports' file: '/shared 192.168.1.100(rw)'. Additionally, administrators can specify wildcard patterns or subnet ranges to allow access from multiple clients or entire networks, such as '/shared 192.168.1.0/24(rw)'. After configuring NFS exports, administrators must restart the NFS server daemon to apply the changes by running the command 'sudo systemctl restart nfs-server' on systemd-based distributions or 'sudo service nfs-kernel-server restart' on SysVinit-based distributions. On the client side, administrators can use the mount command to mount remote NFS exports onto local directories, allowing users to access shared files and directories as if they were stored locally. To mount an NFS export from the server with IP address 192.168.1.10 to the '/mnt/nfs' directory on the client, administrators can use the command 'sudo mount -t nfs 192.168.1.10:/shared /mnt/nfs'. However, securing NFS is critical to prevent unauthorized access to sensitive data and protect against potential security vulnerabilities. By default, NFS does not provide any authentication or encryption mechanisms, making it susceptible to various security threats such as eavesdropping, data tampering, and unauthorized access. To enhance the security of NFS, administrators can implement several security measures, such as configuring NFS access controls, enforcing secure authentication mechanisms, and enabling encryption for data transmission. One of the primary security mechanisms for NFS is to use host-based access controls (HBA), which restrict access to shared directories based on client IP addresses or hostnames specified in the '/etc/exports' file. Administrators can specify allowed client IP addresses or hostnames and their corresponding access permissions, such as read-only or read-write, to control which clients can access the shared directories. Additionally, administrators can use the 'exportfs' command to manage NFS exports and verify the current export configurations. For example, to list all exported directories and their associated configurations, administrators can use the command 'exportfs -v'. Furthermore, administrators can configure NFS to use secure authentication mechanisms such as Kerberos or RPCSEC_GSS to authenticate clients and encrypt data transmission between the NFS server and clients. By enabling Kerberos or RPCSEC_GSS authentication, administrators can ensure that only authenticated and authorized clients can access shared NFS resources and protect sensitive data from unauthorized access or interception. Additionally, administrators can configure NFS to use Transport Layer Security (TLS) or Secure Sockets Layer (SSL) encryption for encrypting data transmission between NFS clients and servers, further enhancing data security and confidentiality. Overall, setting up and securing NFS is essential for enabling efficient file sharing and collaboration in networked environments while protecting sensitive data and ensuring compliance with security requirements. By following best practices for configuring NFS exports, implementing access controls, and enabling secure authentication and encryption mechanisms, administrators can create a robust and secure NFS infrastructure that meets the needs of their organization while mitigating the risk of security breaches and data loss. Configuring network services like DNS (Domain Name System) and DHCP (Dynamic Host Configuration Protocol) is essential for establishing reliable and efficient network communication and ensuring seamless connectivity between devices within a network environment. DNS is a critical network service responsible for translating human-readable domain names into IP addresses, enabling users to access websites, send emails, and communicate with other network resources using easy-to-remember domain names rather than complex IP addresses. DHCP, on the other hand, automates the assignment of IP addresses and network configuration parameters to client devices, simplifying network administration and reducing the burden of manual IP address management. To configure DNS on a Linux system, administrators typically install and configure a DNS server software such as BIND (Berkeley Internet Name Domain), which is one of the most widely used DNS server implementations on Linux systems. BIND provides comprehensive DNS functionality, including domain name resolution, zone management, and DNSSEC (Domain Name System Security Extensions) support. Administrators can install BIND on Debian-based distributions like Ubuntu by running the command 'sudo apt-get install bind9', while on Red Hat-based distributions like CentOS or RHEL, they can use the command 'sudo yum install bind'. Once BIND is installed, administrators can configure DNS zones and records by editing the BIND configuration files located in the '/etc/bind' directory, such as 'named.conf' for global server configuration and 'db.*' files for zone data. For example, to create a new DNS zone for the domain 'example.com' and define DNS records for the domain, administrators can create a new zone configuration file named 'example.com.zone' in the '/etc/bind/zones' directory and add the necessary zone and record definitions. Additionally, administrators can use command-line tools like 'named-checkconf' and 'named-checkzone' to validate the syntax and integrity of BIND configuration files and zone data files, ensuring that the DNS server is properly configured and operational. Similarly, configuring DHCP involves installing and configuring a DHCP server software such as ISC DHCP (Internet Systems Consortium Dynamic Host Configuration Protocol) server, which is the most commonly used DHCP server implementation on Linux systems. ISC DHCP provides robust DHCP functionality, including IP address allocation, lease management, and network configuration options. Administrators can install ISC DHCP on Debian-based distributions like Ubuntu by running the command 'sudo apt-get install isc-dhcp-server', while on Red Hat-based distributions like CentOS or RHEL, they can use the command 'sudo yum install dhcp'. Once ISC DHCP is installed, administrators can configure DHCP server settings by editing the DHCP configuration file located at '/etc/dhcp/dhcpd.conf'. In this configuration file, administrators can define DHCP pools, which specify ranges of IP addresses to be dynamically assigned to client devices, as well as DHCP options, which provide additional configuration parameters such as subnet masks, default gateways, and DNS server addresses. For example, to configure a DHCP pool for the subnet '192.168.1.0/24' with a range of IP addresses from '192.168.1.100' to '192.168.1.200' and specify the DNS server address as '8.8.8.8', administrators can add the following configuration lines to the 'dhcpd.conf' file: 'subnet 192.168.1.0 netmask 255.255.255.0 { range 192.168.1.100 192.168.1.200; option routers 192.168.1.1; option domain-name-servers 8.8.8.8; }'. After configuring DNS and DHCP settings, administrators must restart the respective services to apply the changes by running the command 'sudo systemctl restart bind9' for DNS or 'sudo systemctl restart isc-dhcp-server' for DHCP. Additionally, administrators can use command-line utilities like 'nslookup' or 'dig' to troubleshoot DNS resolution issues and verify DNS server configurations, as well as tools like 'dhcpd' for monitoring DHCP server operations and lease status. Overall, configuring network services like DNS and DHCP is essential for ensuring reliable and efficient network communication, enabling seamless connectivity between devices, and simplifying network administration tasks. By following best practices for configuring and managing DNS and DHCP servers, administrators can create a robust and scalable network infrastructure that meets the needs of their organization while providing reliable and secure network services to users and devices.

Chapter 10: Automating System Tasks with Cron and systemd Timer Units

Advanced cron job scheduling techniques enable administrators to automate complex tasks, manage system resources efficiently, and enhance overall system productivity by leveraging the capabilities of the cron daemon, a time-based job scheduler in Unix-like operating systems. Cron allows users to schedule recurring tasks, execute commands, and run scripts at predefined intervals, providing a powerful mechanism for automating system maintenance, data processing, and other routine operations. While basic cron job scheduling involves specifying the timing parameters for executing a command or script, advanced techniques allow administrators to customize cron jobs further, handle edge cases, and optimize resource usage for improved performance. One advanced technique is the use of cron job chaining, which involves linking multiple cron jobs together to execute a sequence of commands or scripts in a specific order. This technique is useful for orchestrating complex workflows or dependencies between tasks, ensuring that each task completes successfully before the next one begins. To chain cron jobs, administrators can use the && operator to concatenate multiple commands within a single cron job entry, ensuring that each command is executed sequentially and that the entire chain of commands only runs if the previous command succeeds. For example, to execute a series of commands A, B, and C in sequence, administrators can create a cron job entry like this: '0 0 * * * commandA && commandB && commandC', where each command is separated by the && operator, indicating that the next command should only execute if the previous one succeeds. Another advanced technique is the use of cron job templates or parameterized cron jobs, which involve creating reusable cron job definitions with placeholders for parameters that can be customized each time the job is scheduled to run. This technique is particularly useful for automating repetitive tasks with varying input parameters or configurations, such as data processing or report generation tasks. To create a parameterized cron job, administrators can define a shell script or command with placeholders for parameters, then use environment variables or command-line arguments to pass values to the script when scheduling the cron job. For example, suppose administrators have a shell script named 'process_data.sh' that accepts input parameters for processing data files. In that case, they can create a parameterized cron job entry like this: '0 0 * * * /path/to/process_data.sh <input_file> <output_file>', where <input_file> and <output_file> are placeholders for the actual file paths passed as arguments to the script when the cron job runs. Additionally, administrators can use cron job modifiers or advanced scheduling options to define more complex scheduling patterns, such as specifying ranges, intervals, or combinations of specific dates and times for executing cron jobs. These modifiers allow administrators to fine-tune the scheduling behavior of cron jobs and execute them at precise intervals or under specific conditions, such as on weekdays only, during business hours, or on particular days of the month. For example, administrators can use the / syntax to specify intervals for executing cron jobs, such as '/5 * * * *' to run a command every five minutes or '0 0 */2 * *' to run a command every other day. Moreover, administrators can use cron job logging and monitoring tools to track the execution of cron jobs, capture output and errors, and troubleshoot issues effectively. By enabling cron job logging, administrators can ensure accountability, auditability, and visibility into cron job execution, helping them identify and resolve issues promptly and maintain system reliability and availability. To enable cron job logging, administrators can configure the cron daemon to redirect standard output and standard error messages from cron jobs to log files using the '>>' or '2>>' redirection operators in cron job entries. For example, administrators can modify a cron job entry like this: '0 0 * * * /path/to/command >> /var/log/cron.log 2>&1' to redirect both standard output and standard error messages to the '/var/log/cron.log' file for logging and analysis. Furthermore, administrators can use cron job monitoring tools like cronolog or logrotate to rotate and archive cron job log files automatically, preventing log files from growing indefinitely and consuming excessive disk space. These tools allow administrators to manage log files efficiently, compress old log files, and retain historical logs for compliance or troubleshooting purposes. Overall, advanced cron job scheduling techniques enable administrators to automate complex tasks, customize job execution behavior, and monitor cron job execution effectively, enhancing system reliability, efficiency, and maintainability. By leveraging these techniques, administrators can optimize resource usage, streamline operations, and ensure consistent and reliable execution of critical tasks in Unix-like operating environments.

Systemd timer units provide a powerful mechanism for automating tasks and scheduling recurring jobs in Linux systems managed by systemd, the default init system in many modern distributions. Unlike traditional cron jobs, systemd timer units offer more flexibility, reliability, and control over task execution, allowing administrators to define precise scheduling patterns, dependencies, and execution conditions for automated tasks. To create a systemd timer unit, administrators typically create two separate units: a service unit that defines the task or command to be executed and a timer unit that specifies when and how often the task should run. This separation of concerns allows for greater modularity and flexibility in defining and managing automated tasks. To deploy a systemd timer unit, administrators first create a service unit describing the task or command to be executed. They define the task-specific configuration parameters, such as the executable path, command-line arguments, environment variables, and other settings necessary for task execution. For example, suppose administrators want to schedule a daily backup task that creates a compressed archive of specified directories. In that case, they can create a service unit named 'backup.service' with the relevant configuration settings using a text editor like Vim or Nano. Once the service unit is defined, administrators create a corresponding timer unit to schedule the execution of the service unit at specified intervals. They specify the scheduling parameters, such as the initial delay, interval, and accuracy, using systemd timer syntax. For example, to schedule the 'backup.service' unit to run daily at midnight, administrators can create a timer unit named 'backup.timer' with the following configuration: [Unit] Description=Run backup service daily [Timer] OnCalendar=daily Persistent=true [Install] WantedBy=timers.target After defining the service and timer units, administrators must enable and start the timer unit to activate the scheduled task. They use the 'systemctl enable' command to enable the timer unit, ensuring that it starts automatically at boot time, and the 'systemctl start' command to start the timer unit immediately. For example, administrators can enable and start the 'backup.timer' unit using the following commands: systemctl enable backup.timer systemctl start backup.timer Once the timer unit is enabled and started, systemd automatically triggers the associated service unit according to the specified schedule, executing the defined task or command at the specified intervals. Administrators can monitor the status and execution logs of systemd timer units using the 'systemctl status' and 'journalctl' commands, respectively. They can view detailed information about the timer unit, including the next scheduled run time, the time remaining until the next run, and any recent execution logs or errors. Additionally, administrators can adjust the scheduling parameters of systemd timer units dynamically using the 'systemctl' command. They can modify the timer unit configuration, such as changing the scheduling interval or adjusting the accuracy, and reload the systemd configuration to apply the changes immediately. For example, administrators can use the following commands to modify the scheduling parameters of the 'backup.timer' unit and reload the systemd configuration: systemctl edit backup.timer systemctl daemon-reload systemd timer units also support advanced scheduling features, such as calendar-based scheduling, monotonic timers, and random delays, allowing administrators to define complex scheduling patterns and conditions for automated tasks. Calendar-based scheduling allows administrators to specify task execution times using calendar events, such as specific dates, days of the week, or times of the day, providing greater flexibility in defining recurring schedules. Monotonic timers ensure accurate and consistent task execution intervals, even in cases of system time changes or adjustments, by measuring time elapsed since the timer was last started or activated. Random delays introduce variability into task execution times, preventing system overload and resource contention by spreading out task execution over time. By leveraging these advanced scheduling features, administrators can optimize resource usage, reduce system load, and improve task execution efficiency in systemd-managed environments. In summary, systemd timer units offer a robust and flexible solution for automating tasks and scheduling recurring jobs in Linux systems. With their powerful features, such as precise scheduling, dependency management, and dynamic configuration, systemd timer units provide administrators with the tools they need to automate routine tasks effectively, ensuring system reliability, efficiency, and maintainability.

BOOK 3

RHCSA EXAM PASS

NETWORK ADMINISTRATION AND SECURITY

ROB BOTWRIGHT

Chapter 1: Introduction to Networking Fundamentals

Understanding the basic concepts of computer networking is fundamental for anyone delving into the world of IT, as networking forms the backbone of modern communication and connectivity. At its core, computer networking involves the interconnection of devices, such as computers, servers, routers, switches, and other hardware components, to enable data exchange and resource sharing across a network. Networks can vary in size and complexity, ranging from small, local networks within a home or office to large-scale, global networks spanning multiple continents. One of the key components of computer networking is the transmission medium, which refers to the physical or wireless means by which data is transmitted between devices on a network. Common transmission media include copper wires, fiber optic cables, and wireless radio frequencies, each with its own advantages and limitations in terms of speed, distance, and reliability. In addition to the transmission medium, computer networks rely on network protocols, which are sets of rules and conventions that govern how data is formatted, transmitted, received, and interpreted by devices on the network. Protocols define standards for communication, addressing, error detection and correction, routing, and other network functions, ensuring interoperability and compatibility between different devices and systems. One of the most widely used network protocols is the Internet Protocol (IP), which provides addressing and routing capabilities for data packets on the Internet and other TCP/IP (Transmission Control Protocol/Internet Protocol) networks. IP addresses uniquely identify devices on a network and facilitate the delivery of data packets to their intended destinations across interconnected networks. Another essential protocol is the Transmission Control Protocol (TCP), which operates at a higher level than IP and provides reliable, connection-oriented communication between devices by establishing virtual connections, sequencing data packets, and implementing flow control mechanisms. Together, IP and TCP form the foundation of the Internet and many other networked systems, enabling reliable and efficient communication between devices worldwide. In addition to IP and TCP, computer networks often use other protocols and technologies to support specific network services and applications, such as the Domain Name System (DNS) for translating domain names into IP addresses, the Hypertext Transfer Protocol (HTTP) for accessing web pages and resources, and the Simple Mail Transfer Protocol (SMTP) for sending email messages. These protocols work together to provide a rich and diverse set of network services and applications that enable users to communicate, collaborate, and access information across networks. Beyond protocols, computer networks also rely on network topologies, which define the physical or logical layout of devices and connections within a network. Common network topologies include bus, star, ring, mesh, and hybrid topologies, each with its own advantages and disadvantages in terms of scalability, fault tolerance, and performance. Administrators can deploy these topologies to design and configure networks that meet specific requirements for connectivity, reliability, and performance. Moreover, computer networks employ network devices and components, such as routers, switches, hubs, and access points, to facilitate communication and data transfer between devices on a network. Routers are responsible for forwarding data packets between different networks, while switches and hubs enable communication between devices within the same network segment. Access points provide wireless connectivity for devices to connect to a wireless network. Each of these devices plays a crucial role in ensuring the smooth operation and performance of computer networks. Lastly, network security is a critical consideration in computer networking, as networks are vulnerable to various security threats, such as unauthorized access, data breaches, malware infections, and denial-of-service attacks. Administrators employ a range of security measures, including firewalls, intrusion detection and prevention systems (IDPS), encryption, authentication, and access control, to protect network resources, data, and users from security breaches and cyber threats. By implementing robust security measures and adhering to best practices, organizations can safeguard their networks and mitigate the risks posed by potential security threats. In summary, understanding the basic concepts of computer networking is essential for building, configuring, and maintaining modern networks that enable communication, collaboration, and access to resources across diverse computing environments. From transmission media and network protocols to topologies, devices, and security considerations, each aspect of computer networking contributes to the design, operation,

and security of interconnected systems that power today's digital world.
An overview of network components and topologies is essential for understanding the structure and functionality of computer networks, which serve as the foundation for modern communication and connectivity. Network components encompass a variety of hardware and software elements that work together to facilitate data transmission, resource sharing, and communication between devices on a network. Common network components include devices such as routers, switches, hubs, access points, network interface cards (NICs), cables, and network operating systems (NOS). Each of these components plays a specific role in enabling network communication and connectivity. Routers are critical network devices that forward data packets between different networks, allowing devices on separate networks to communicate with each other. Switches, on the other hand, are used to connect devices within the same network segment and facilitate the efficient transfer of data between devices. Hubs are simpler devices that connect multiple devices in a network, but they operate at a lower level than switches and do not perform packet switching. Access points provide wireless connectivity for devices to

connect to a wireless network, allowing for flexible and convenient access to network resources. Network interface cards (NICs) are hardware components installed in computers and other devices to enable them to connect to a network, either wired or wirelessly. Cables, such as Ethernet cables and fiber optic cables, are used to physically connect devices to a network and transmit data between them. Network operating systems (NOS) are specialized software that manages network resources, configures network settings, and facilitates communication between devices on a network. These components work together to form the infrastructure of computer networks and enable the exchange of data and information between devices. In addition to network components, network topologies define the physical or logical layout of devices and connections within a network. Common network topologies include bus, star, ring, mesh, and hybrid topologies, each with its own characteristics, advantages, and disadvantages. A bus topology consists of a single shared communication medium, to which all devices are connected, forming a linear network. In a star topology, devices are connected to a central hub or switch, facilitating efficient communication between devices and allowing for easy expansion of the network. A ring topology connects devices in a closed loop, with each device connected to two other devices, forming a circular network. A mesh topology connects devices in a fully interconnected manner, with each device connected to every other device in the network, providing redundancy and fault tolerance. Hybrid topologies combine two or more basic topologies to create a more flexible and scalable network infrastructure. Administrators can choose the most appropriate network topology based on factors such as the size of the network, the level of redundancy required, the ease of maintenance, and the cost considerations. To deploy a network topology, administrators must physically or logically connect devices according to the chosen topology and configure network settings accordingly. For example, to set up a star topology, administrators would connect all devices to a central hub or switch using Ethernet cables and configure the network devices to communicate with each other. They may also need to configure IP addresses, subnet masks, and other network settings to ensure proper communication and connectivity between devices. By understanding the different network components and topologies available, administrators can design and deploy efficient and reliable network infrastructures that meet the communication and connectivity needs of their organizations. Whether building a small office network or a large-scale enterprise network, careful consideration of network components and topologies is essential for ensuring optimal performance, scalability, and reliability.

Chapter 2: Understanding TCP/IP Protocol Suite

Understanding TCP/IP layers and protocols is crucial for comprehending how data is transmitted, routed, and received across networks, as TCP/IP serves as the foundation for communication on the Internet and many other computer networks. TCP/IP, which stands for Transmission Control Protocol/Internet Protocol, is a suite of networking protocols that provides reliable, end-to-end communication between devices on a network. The TCP/IP protocol suite is organized into four layers: the Application layer, the Transport layer, the Internet layer, and the Link layer, each with its own set of protocols and functions. Starting from the top, the Application layer is responsible for providing network services to applications running on devices, such as web browsers, email clients, and file transfer utilities. Common protocols at the Application layer include HTTP (Hypertext Transfer Protocol) for web browsing, SMTP (Simple Mail Transfer Protocol) for sending email, and FTP (File Transfer Protocol) for transferring files. These protocols define the rules and conventions for communication between applications and ensure interoperability across different software and platforms. Moving down the stack, the Transport layer is responsible for end-to-end communication between devices and provides mechanisms for data segmentation, flow control, error detection, and error correction. The two primary protocols at the Transport layer are TCP (Transmission Control Protocol) and UDP (User Datagram Protocol). TCP is connection-oriented and provides reliable, error-checked delivery of data packets, making it suitable for applications that require guaranteed delivery, such as web browsing and email. UDP, on the other hand, is connectionless and does not provide error checking or reliable delivery but offers lower overhead and faster transmission speeds, making it ideal for real-time communication applications, such as streaming media and online gaming. Beneath the Transport layer lies the Internet layer, which is responsible for routing data packets between devices on different networks and facilitating internetwork communication. The primary protocol at the Internet layer is IP (Internet Protocol), which provides addressing, routing, and fragmentation of data packets. IP addresses uniquely identify devices on a network and allow routers to forward data packets to their intended destinations across interconnected networks. Additionally, the

Internet Control Message Protocol (ICMP) operates at the Internet layer and is used for diagnostic and error reporting purposes, such as ping and traceroute. At the lowest level of the TCP/IP protocol stack is the Link layer, also known as the Network Interface layer or the Data Link layer, which is responsible for transmitting data packets between directly connected devices on the same network segment. Common protocols at the Link layer include Ethernet, Wi-Fi (IEEE 802.11), and PPP (Point-to-Point Protocol). These protocols define the rules for addressing, framing, and error detection at the physical and data link layers of the OSI model. Administrators can use various CLI commands to configure and manage TCP/IP protocols and settings on network devices. For example, the 'ipconfig' command in Windows and the 'ifconfig' command in Unix-like operating systems can be used to display network interface configuration information, including IP addresses, subnet masks, and gateway addresses. Similarly, the 'ping' command can be used to test network connectivity by sending ICMP echo requests to a remote host and waiting for an ICMP echo reply. Additionally, the 'netstat' command can be used to display active network connections, routing tables, and network statistics. By understanding the TCP/IP layers and protocols and how they interact with each other, administrators can troubleshoot network issues, optimize network performance, and design scalable and reliable network architectures that meet the communication needs of their organizations. TCP/IP addressing and subnetting are fundamental concepts in computer networking, essential for the proper functioning and organization of IP-based networks. IP addresses serve as unique identifiers for devices connected to a network, allowing them to communicate with each other across the Internet and other TCP/IP networks. An IP address consists of a series of binary digits, typically represented in decimal format, and is divided into two parts: the network portion and the host portion. The network portion identifies the network to which a device belongs, while the host portion identifies the specific device on that network. IPv4, the most widely used version of the Internet Protocol, uses 32-bit addresses, divided into four octets separated by periods. For example, the IP address 192.168.0.1 consists of four octets, each representing a decimal value ranging from 0 to 255. IPv6, the next generation of the Internet Protocol, uses 128-bit addresses, represented in hexadecimal format and separated by colons. Subnetting is the process of dividing a large IP network into smaller, more manageable subnetworks, or subnets, to improve network efficiency and manageability. Subnetting allows administrators to allocate IP addresses more efficiently, reduce network congestion, and enhance security by isolating different parts of the network from each other. Subnetting involves borrowing bits from the host portion of an IP address to create additional network prefixes, effectively dividing a network into multiple smaller subnets. To subnet an IP network, administrators need to determine the appropriate subnet mask, which defines the boundary between the network portion and the host portion of an IP address. The subnet mask consists of a series of binary digits, typically represented in decimal format, and determines the size of each subnet and the number of available host addresses within each subnet. Common subnet masks include /24 (255.255.255.0), /16 (255.255.0.0), and /8 (255.0.0.0), which correspond to Class C, Class B, and Class A networks, respectively. For example, a subnet mask of /24 divides an IPv4 network into 256 subnets, each capable of accommodating up to 254 host addresses. Administrators can use CLI commands such as 'ipcalc' or 'subnetcalc' to calculate subnet masks and determine the appropriate subnetting scheme for their networks. Once the subnet mask is determined, administrators can allocate IP addresses to devices within each subnet, ensuring that each device has a unique IP address and that all devices on the same subnet can communicate with each other. Subnetting also enables administrators to implement network segmentation and security policies by isolating different parts of the network into separate subnets and applying access control rules and firewall policies to control traffic between subnets. By subnetting their networks, administrators can optimize network performance, improve scalability, and enhance security, ensuring that their networks can meet the demands of modern computing environments.

Chapter 3: Configuring Network Interfaces and Routing

Network interface configuration is a crucial aspect of setting up and managing computer networks, as it involves configuring network interfaces on devices to enable communication and connectivity. A network interface, also known as a network adapter or network card, is a hardware component that allows a device to connect to a network and transmit data. Network interfaces can be wired or wireless and come in various forms, such as Ethernet adapters, Wi-Fi cards, and cellular modems. Configuring network interfaces involves assigning IP addresses, subnet masks, default gateways, and other network settings to enable communication with other devices on the network and access to the Internet. In Unix-like operating systems, the 'ifconfig' command is commonly used to configure network interfaces, display interface configuration information, and manage network settings. For example, to assign an IP address to a network interface, administrators can use the 'ifconfig' command followed by the name of the interface and the desired IP address, subnet mask, and other parameters. Similarly, the 'ip' command can be used to configure network interfaces in Linux systems, providing a more modern and flexible alternative to 'ifconfig'. For Windows operating systems, the 'ipconfig' command is used to display network interface configuration information, including IP addresses, subnet masks, default gateways, and DNS servers. Additionally, the 'netsh' command can be used to configure network interfaces and modify network settings, such as enabling or disabling DHCP (Dynamic Host Configuration Protocol) and setting static IP addresses. Network interface configuration also involves configuring advanced network settings, such as DNS (Domain Name System) servers, WINS (Windows Internet Name Service) servers, and VLAN (Virtual Local Area Network) tagging. DNS servers translate domain names into IP addresses, allowing devices to locate and communicate with servers on the Internet using human-readable domain names. Administrators can specify DNS server addresses in network interface configuration settings to ensure that devices can resolve domain names to IP addresses and access Internet resources. Similarly, WINS servers provide a centralized database for mapping NetBIOS names to IP addresses in Windows networks, enabling devices to locate and communicate with each other using NetBIOS names. VLAN tagging allows administrators to partition a physical network into multiple logical networks, or VLANs, by adding VLAN tags to network frames, which contain information about the VLAN membership of the frame. VLAN tagging is commonly used in enterprise networks to improve network security, optimize network performance, and simplify network management by isolating different types of traffic and applying different security policies to each VLAN. In addition to basic network interface configuration, administrators must also configure network settings such as default gateways, which are used to route traffic between different networks, and subnet masks, which determine the size of the network and the range of IP addresses available for assignment. By configuring network interfaces and settings correctly, administrators can ensure that devices can communicate with each other effectively and access network resources and the Internet without encountering connectivity issues or security vulnerabilities.

Routing configuration is a critical aspect of managing computer networks, enabling devices to communicate with each other across interconnected networks by determining the optimal path for data packets to reach their destinations. Routing involves directing network traffic between different networks based on destination IP addresses, using routing tables and routing protocols to determine the best path for each packet. In many cases, routers use dynamic routing protocols to automatically exchange routing information and update their routing tables in real-time based on network topology changes. However, in some situations, administrators may need to configure static routes manually to define specific paths for network traffic. A static route is a pre-defined entry in a router's routing table that specifies the next hop or outgoing interface for packets destined for a particular network or IP address range. Static routes are commonly used to route traffic between networks that do not change frequently or to override dynamic routing decisions for specific destinations. To configure a static route on a router, administrators can use the 'route' command in Unix-like operating systems or the 'ip route' command in Linux systems. For example, to add a static route to the 192.168.2.0/24 network via the gateway 192.168.1.1, administrators can use the command 'route add -net 192.168.2.0/24 gw 192.168.1.1'. Similarly, in Windows operating systems, administrators can use the 'route' command to add static routes to the routing table. For example, to add a static route to the 192.168.2.0/24 network via the gateway 192.168.1.1, administrators can use the command 'route add 192.168.2.0 mask 255.255.255.0 192.168.1.1'. When configuring static routes, administrators must ensure that the specified next hop or outgoing interface is reachable and properly configured to forward packets to the intended destination. Additionally, administrators should consider the network topology and traffic patterns to determine the most efficient routing configuration for their networks. Static routes can be used to implement policy-based routing, where traffic is forwarded along specific paths based on predefined criteria, such as source IP address, destination IP address, or packet attributes. Policy-based routing allows administrators to control and manipulate network traffic flows to meet specific requirements, such as load balancing, traffic shaping, and traffic prioritization. Static routes can also be used to implement backup or redundant paths for critical network traffic, ensuring high availability and fault tolerance in the event of link failures or network outages. By configuring static routes strategically, administrators can optimize network performance, improve network reliability, and ensure efficient routing of traffic between interconnected networks. However, it's essential to monitor and maintain static routes regularly to accommodate changes in network topology or traffic patterns and avoid routing issues or suboptimal performance. Administrators can use network monitoring tools and routing protocols to detect and troubleshoot routing problems, such as routing loops, black-holing, and asymmetric routing, and adjust static routes as needed to ensure smooth and reliable network operation.

Chapter 4: DNS Configuration and Management

Domain Name System (DNS) is a fundamental component of the Internet infrastructure, serving as the distributed hierarchical system that translates human-readable domain names into numerical IP addresses. DNS plays a crucial role in facilitating communication between devices on the Internet by providing a way to locate and identify resources using meaningful domain names instead of complex IP addresses. At its core, DNS operates as a distributed database organized into a hierarchical structure, consisting of multiple levels of domain names arranged in a tree-like hierarchy. Each domain name corresponds to a specific IP address or set of IP addresses, allowing users to access websites, send emails, and connect to other network resources using simple, easy-to-remember domain names. The DNS hierarchy begins with the root domain, represented by a single dot ('.') and serving as the top-level of the DNS hierarchy. Below the root domain are the top-level domains (TLDs), which include generic TLDs such as .com, .net, .org, as well as country-code TLDs such as .us, .uk, .de, each managed by a designated registry organization. Beneath the TLDs are second-level domains (SLDs), which are the main part of a domain name, followed by optional subdomains, separated by periods ('.'). For example, in the domain name example.com, 'example' is the SLD, and 'com' is the TLD. DNS operates using a client-server architecture, with DNS clients, such as web browsers, email clients, and other network applications, sending DNS queries to DNS servers to resolve domain names into IP addresses. DNS servers are responsible for storing and maintaining DNS records, which map domain names to IP addresses and vice versa, and responding to DNS queries from clients. There are several types of DNS records used to store different types of information in the DNS database, including A records, which map domain names to IPv4 addresses, AAAA records, which map domain names to IPv6 addresses, MX records, which specify the mail servers responsible for receiving email for a domain, and CNAME records, which provide aliases for domain names. DNS resolution process begins when a DNS client sends a DNS query to its configured DNS resolver, typically a recursive resolver provided by the Internet service provider (ISP) or a public DNS resolver such as Google DNS or Cloudflare DNS. The resolver then forwards the query to the root DNS servers, which respond with a referral to the appropriate TLD DNS servers responsible for the requested domain name. The resolver then sends a query to the TLD DNS servers, which respond with a referral to the authoritative DNS servers for the requested domain. Finally, the resolver sends a query to the authoritative DNS servers, which respond with the requested DNS records, allowing the resolver to complete the DNS resolution process and return the IP address to the client. DNS also supports caching to improve performance and reduce the load on DNS servers by temporarily storing DNS records in memory or on disk. When a DNS resolver receives a response to a DNS query, it caches the response for a configurable period, known as the time-to-live (TTL), allowing subsequent queries for the same domain name to be answered more quickly without needing to query authoritative DNS servers again. DNS caching helps reduce latency and improve the overall efficiency of the DNS resolution process, especially for frequently accessed domain names. DNS is a critical component of Internet communication, providing a reliable and scalable mechanism for translating domain names into IP addresses and enabling seamless access to network resources. However, DNS is also a

potential target for malicious activities, such as DNS spoofing, DNS cache poisoning, and DNS amplification attacks, which can disrupt network communication and compromise the security and integrity of DNS data. As such, it's essential for network administrators to implement best practices for securing DNS infrastructure, including deploying DNSSEC (DNS Security Extensions) to provide data origin authentication and data integrity protection for DNS records, implementing DNS filtering to block access to malicious domains and prevent malware infections, and regularly monitoring and auditing DNS traffic and DNS server logs for signs of suspicious activity or unauthorized access. By understanding the fundamentals of DNS and implementing appropriate security measures, organizations can ensure the reliability, availability, and security of their DNS infrastructure and maintain smooth and secure Internet connectivity for their users.
DNS server configuration and zone management are essential aspects of maintaining a functional and reliable Domain Name System (DNS) infrastructure, ensuring that DNS servers are properly configured to handle DNS queries and resolve domain names into IP addresses accurately. DNS servers can be configured to serve

different types of DNS zones, including forward lookup zones, reverse lookup zones, and conditional forwarders, each serving a specific purpose in the DNS resolution process. To configure a DNS server on a Linux system, administrators can use BIND (Berkeley Internet Name Domain), the most widely used DNS server software on the Internet, or other DNS server software such as NSD (Name Server Daemon) or PowerDNS. In Windows Server environments, administrators can use the DNS Server role included with Windows Server operating systems, which provides a comprehensive set of features and tools for DNS server configuration and management. The first step in DNS server configuration is to install the DNS server software on the server system using the appropriate package management tools or server management interfaces. Once installed, administrators can configure the DNS server settings, including network interfaces, listening ports, and resolver options, using configuration files or graphical user interfaces provided by the DNS server software. In BIND, DNS server configuration is typically done using the named.conf configuration file located in the /etc/bind/ directory, where administrators can specify global options, zone definitions, and other server settings. For example, to configure BIND to listen for DNS queries on specific network interfaces and IP addresses, administrators can edit the named.conf file and add 'listen-on' directives for each interface, specifying the IP address and port number to listen on. Similarly, in Windows Server environments, administrators can use the DNS Manager console to configure DNS server settings, including server properties, forwarders, root hints, and other options. Once the DNS server is configured, administrators can create and manage DNS zones to store DNS records for domain names and IP addresses within their organization's DNS namespace. A DNS zone is a portion of the DNS namespace for which a particular DNS server is authoritative, meaning that the server is responsible for storing and maintaining DNS records for the zone and responding to DNS queries for domain names within the zone. To create a new DNS zone, administrators can use the appropriate administrative tools provided by the DNS server software or use command-line interface (CLI) commands to create zone files manually. In BIND, administrators can create a new forward lookup zone by adding a zone definition to the named.conf file, specifying the zone name, zone type, and other zone options. For example, to create a new forward lookup zone for the domain example.com, administrators can add a zone definition like the following to the named.conf file: 'zone "example.com" { type master; file "/etc/bind/zones/example.com.zone"; };'. Similarly, in Windows Server environments, administrators can use the DNS Manager console to create new forward lookup zones by right-clicking on the Forward Lookup Zones folder and selecting the New Zone option from the context menu, then following the wizard to specify the zone name, zone type, and other zone settings. Once the DNS zone is created, administrators can add DNS records to the zone to define mappings between domain names and IP addresses and other resource records such as mail exchanger (MX) records, canonical name (CNAME) records, and service (SRV) records. DNS records can be added using administrative tools provided by the DNS server software or by editing zone files manually using a text editor. In BIND, DNS records are typically stored in zone files located in the /etc/bind/zones/ directory, where each zone file corresponds to a specific DNS zone and contains DNS records in a standard text-based format. For example, a zone file for the example.com forward lookup zone might contain DNS records like the following: '@ IN SOA ns1.example.com.

admin.example.com. (2022010101 ; serial number 3600 ; refresh 1800 ; retry 604800 ; expire 86400 ; minimum TTL) ; NS Records IN NS ns1.example.com. IN NS ns2.example.com. ; A Records ns1 IN A 192.168.1.10 ns2 IN A 192.168.1.11 ; MX Record IN MX 10 mail.example.com. ; CNAME Record www IN CNAME example.com. ; PTR Records 10 IN PTR ns1.example.com. 11 IN PTR ns2.example.com.'. Similarly, in Windows Server environments, administrators can use the DNS Manager console to add new DNS records to a zone by right-clicking on the zone name and selecting the New Record option from the context menu, then following the wizard to specify the record type, name, data, and other record settings. Once DNS records are added to the zone, the DNS server is ready to respond to DNS queries for domain names within the zone, providing accurate and reliable DNS resolution services to clients on the network. DNS server configuration and zone management are ongoing tasks that require regular maintenance and monitoring to ensure the integrity, availability, and security of the DNS infrastructure. Administrators should regularly review DNS server settings, monitor DNS server performance and availability, and audit DNS zone configurations to detect and resolve issues proactively. By following best practices for DNS server configuration and zone management, administrators can ensure that their DNS infrastructure remains robust, resilient, and responsive to the needs of their organization's network environment.

Chapter 5: DHCP Configuration and Troubleshooting

Dynamic Host Configuration Protocol (DHCP) is a network protocol used to automate the assignment of IP addresses and other network configuration parameters to devices on a TCP/IP network, simplifying the process of network administration and management. DHCP allows devices to obtain IP addresses dynamically from a DHCP server instead of requiring manual configuration, enabling seamless connectivity and efficient resource utilization in large-scale network environments. The DHCP protocol operates on a client-server model, with DHCP clients requesting network configuration parameters from DHCP servers and DHCP servers responding with lease offers containing IP address assignments and other configuration information. DHCP clients include devices such as computers, smartphones, tablets, and other network-enabled devices that require network connectivity, while DHCP servers are responsible for allocating and managing IP addresses and other network configuration parameters for DHCP clients within a network. DHCP servers can be implemented using dedicated DHCP server software such as ISC DHCP (Internet Systems Consortium Dynamic Host Configuration Protocol), which is the most widely used DHCP server software on Unix-like operating systems, or Microsoft DHCP Server, which is included with Windows Server operating systems and provides DHCP services in Windows-based network environments. To configure a DHCP server using ISC DHCP on a Unix-like operating system such as Linux or FreeBSD, administrators can install the ISC DHCP package using the appropriate package management tools for their distribution, such as apt, yum, or pkg. Once installed, administrators can configure the DHCP server settings, including network interfaces, IP address pools, lease durations, and DHCP options, using configuration files located in the /etc/dhcp/ directory. For example, to configure a DHCP server to listen for DHCP client requests on a specific network interface and subnet, administrators can edit the dhcpd.conf configuration file and define a subnet declaration for the desired subnet, specifying the subnet address, subnet mask, and DHCP options. In Microsoft Windows Server environments, administrators can configure the DHCP Server role using the DHCP Manager console, which provides a graphical user interface for managing DHCP server settings, IP address pools, DHCP scopes, and other configuration options. Once the DHCP server is configured, DHCP clients can obtain IP addresses and other network configuration parameters by sending DHCP discover messages to the local network broadcast address, requesting DHCP lease offers from available DHCP servers. DHCP servers respond to DHCP client requests by sending DHCP offer messages containing IP address assignments and other configuration information, which DHCP clients can accept by sending DHCP request messages to the selected DHCP server. Once a DHCP lease offer is accepted by a DHCP client, the DHCP server assigns the IP address to the client and updates its lease database to track the lease duration and other lease parameters. DHCP clients then configure their network interfaces with the assigned IP address and other configuration parameters, allowing them to communicate with other devices on the network. DHCP leases are temporary and have a finite duration, typically ranging from a few hours to several days, after which DHCP clients must renew their leases by sending DHCP request messages to the DHCP server. If a DHCP client fails to renew its lease before it expires, the DHCP server can reclaim the IP address and lease it to another client, ensuring efficient utilization of available IP address space. DHCP also supports the allocation of other network configuration parameters to DHCP clients, such as subnet masks, default gateways, DNS server addresses, and domain names, allowing DHCP clients to configure their network interfaces automatically with the necessary information to communicate on the network. DHCP options are configurable parameters that can be included in DHCP lease offers and requests to provide additional network configuration settings to DHCP clients, such as NTP server addresses, WINS server addresses, and vendor-specific options. DHCP relay agents can be used to extend DHCP services across multiple network segments or subnets by forwarding DHCP messages between DHCP clients and DHCP servers located on different network segments. DHCP relay agents listen for DHCP client requests on local network interfaces and forward the requests to one or more configured DHCP servers, which respond with DHCP lease offers that are relayed back to the requesting DHCP clients. By deploying DHCP relay agents strategically within a network infrastructure, administrators can centralize DHCP services and manage IP address allocation efficiently across large-scale network environments. DHCP plays a critical role in simplifying network administration and management, providing a flexible and scalable solution for automatically assigning IP addresses and other network configuration parameters to devices on TCP/IP networks. By configuring DHCP servers and DHCP clients appropriately and monitoring DHCP lease activity regularly, administrators can ensure the reliable and efficient operation of DHCP services in their network environments, supporting seamless connectivity and optimal resource utilization for end users and network applications.

DHCP (Dynamic Host Configuration Protocol) server configuration is essential for automating the assignment of IP addresses and other network configuration parameters to devices on a TCP/IP network. Configuring a DHCP server involves setting up and managing IP address pools, lease durations, DHCP options, and other settings to ensure seamless connectivity for DHCP clients. One popular DHCP server software is ISC DHCP (Internet Systems Consortium DHCP), which is widely used in Unix-like operating systems such as Linux and FreeBSD. To install ISC DHCP on a Linux system, you can use package management tools like apt, yum, or dnf, depending on your Linux distribution. For example, on Debian-based systems like Ubuntu, you can use the apt package manager to install ISC DHCP by running the command "sudo apt install isc-dhcp-server". After installing ISC DHCP, you need to configure the DHCP server settings by editing the dhcpd.conf configuration file located in the /etc/dhcp/ directory. The dhcpd.conf file contains configuration directives that define DHCP server parameters such as subnet declarations, IP address pools, lease durations, DHCP options, and DHCP client settings. To create a basic DHCP server configuration, you can define a subnet declaration for the network segment that the DHCP server serves and specify the subnet address and subnet mask. For example, to configure a DHCP server for the 192.168.1.0/24 network segment, you can add the following subnet declaration to the dhcpd.conf file:

bash

Copy code

```
subnet 192.168.1.0 netmask 255.255.255.0 { # DHCP server configuration directives go here }
```

Inside the subnet declaration, you can configure DHCP options such as the default gateway, DNS server addresses, domain name, and lease duration. For example, to specify the default gateway and DNS server addresses for DHCP clients, you can use the "option routers" and "option domain-name-servers" directives, respectively. Additionally, you can define an IP address pool using the "range" directive to specify the range of IP addresses that the DHCP server can allocate to DHCP clients. Once you have configured the dhcpd.conf file, you can start the DHCP server using the appropriate service management command for your Linux distribution. For example, on systemd-based systems like Ubuntu 18.04 and later, you can start the DHCP server using the systemctl command:

sql

Copy code

```
sudo systemctl start isc-dhcp-server
```

To enable the DHCP server to start automatically at boot time, you can use the systemctl enable command:

bash

Copy code

```
sudo systemctl enable isc-dhcp-server
```

After starting the DHCP server, you can monitor its status and view log messages to troubleshoot any issues that may arise during operation. The DHCP server logs are typically located in the /var/log/syslog file on Debian-based systems or /var/log/messages file on Red Hat-based systems. You can use the tail command to view the last few lines of the DHCP server log file and grep command to filter log messages based on specific criteria. For example, to view DHCP server log messages related to DHCP lease assignments, you can use the following command:

bash

Copy code

```
tail -f /var/log/syslog | grep DHCPACK
```

This command will display real-time log messages from the DHCP server log file that contain the string "DHCPACK", indicating successful DHCP lease assignments to DHCP clients. In addition to monitoring DHCP server logs, you can use diagnostic tools like tcpdump or Wireshark to capture and analyze DHCP network traffic between DHCP clients and the DHCP server. These tools allow you to inspect DHCP messages exchanged between clients and the server, identify communication issues, and troubleshoot DHCP configuration problems. For example, you can use the tcpdump command to capture DHCP traffic on a specific network interface and save the captured packets to a file for analysis:

css

Copy code

```
sudo tcpdump -i eth0 -n udp port 67 or udp port 68 -w dhcp.pcap
```

This command captures DHCP traffic on the eth0 network interface and writes the captured packets to a file named dhcp.pcap in pcap format, which can be opened and analyzed using Wireshark or other packet analysis tools. By monitoring DHCP server logs and analyzing DHCP network traffic, you can identify and resolve DHCP configuration issues, troubleshoot connectivity problems, and ensure reliable operation of DHCP services in your network environment.

Chapter 6: Implementing VLANs and Network Segmentation

VLANs (Virtual Local Area Networks) are a fundamental concept in modern network design, allowing administrators to segment a physical network into multiple logical networks for improved performance, security, and manageability. VLANs are commonly used in enterprise networks to isolate traffic, optimize network resources, and enhance network scalability. To understand VLANs, it's essential to grasp the concept of network segmentation, which involves dividing a single physical network into multiple logical networks based on criteria such as department, function, or security requirements. VLANs achieve network segmentation by assigning VLAN tags to network frames, indicating the VLAN membership of each frame and enabling switches to forward traffic between VLANs based on VLAN membership. The VLAN tagging process adds a VLAN tag to each Ethernet frame as it traverses the network, allowing switches to differentiate between traffic belonging to different VLANs and enforce VLAN-based policies. In VLAN terminology, a VLAN tag is known as a VLAN ID or VLAN number, which is a unique numeric identifier assigned to each VLAN in the network. VLANs are identified by VLAN IDs ranging from 1 to 4096, with certain VLAN IDs reserved for specific purposes such as VLAN 1 for the default VLAN and VLANs 1002 to 1005 for legacy Token Ring VLANs. VLAN configuration involves several key steps, including VLAN creation, VLAN assignment, and VLAN trunking. To create a VLAN on a network switch, administrators can use the switch's command-line interface (CLI) or web-based management interface to access the switch's configuration settings and create a new VLAN. For example, on a Cisco Catalyst switch, you can create a VLAN using the following CLI command:

php

Copy code

```
vlan <vlan-id>
```

This command creates a new VLAN with the specified VLAN ID on the switch. Once a VLAN is created, administrators can assign switch ports to the VLAN to control which devices are members of the VLAN and regulate traffic flow between VLANs. Port assignment can be done manually by configuring individual switch ports or dynamically using VLAN trunking protocols such as IEEE 802.1Q or Cisco's proprietary VLAN Trunking

Protocol (VTP). VLAN trunking enables switches to carry traffic for multiple VLANs over a single physical link, allowing for efficient use of network bandwidth and simplifying VLAN deployment. To configure VLAN trunking on a switch port, administrators can use the following CLI command:

Copy code

```
switchport mode trunk
```

This command configures the switch port to operate in trunk mode, allowing it to carry traffic for multiple VLANs. Additionally, administrators can specify which VLANs are allowed to traverse the trunk link using the "switchport trunk allowed vlan" command followed by a list of VLAN IDs. VLANs can also be configured with additional parameters such as VLAN names, VLAN membership modes, VLAN interfaces, and VLAN tagging protocols. VLAN membership modes include access mode, which assigns a single VLAN to a switch port, and trunk mode, which allows the switch port to carry traffic for multiple VLANs. VLAN interfaces, also known as SVIs (Switched Virtual Interfaces), are virtual interfaces configured on Layer 3 switches to provide routing between VLANs. To configure a VLAN interface on a Layer 3 switch, administrators can use the following CLI command:

csharp
Copy code

```
interface vlan <vlan-id>
```

This command creates a VLAN interface with the specified VLAN ID on the switch, allowing for inter-VLAN routing and communication between VLANs. VLAN tagging protocols such as IEEE 802.1Q are used to encapsulate VLAN information in Ethernet frames and facilitate VLAN identification and segregation across network devices. VLAN tagging adds a VLAN tag to each Ethernet frame, indicating the VLAN membership of the frame and allowing switches to forward traffic between VLANs based on VLAN tags. VLANs offer several benefits for network administration and management, including improved network performance, enhanced security, simplified network configuration, and increased flexibility. By segmenting the network into smaller logical networks, VLANs help reduce broadcast traffic, optimize network resources, and isolate network traffic for improved security and compliance. Additionally, VLANs enable administrators to implement network policies and access controls based on VLAN membership, restricting access to sensitive network resources and applications. VLANs can also facilitate network design and expansion by providing a scalable and flexible framework for adding, modifying, and removing network segments as needed. Overall, VLANs are a fundamental building block of modern network design, offering a versatile and powerful solution for organizing and managing network traffic in diverse IT environments.

Network segmentation is a crucial aspect of modern network design, allowing organizations to enhance security, optimize performance, and improve manageability by dividing their networks into smaller, isolated segments. One of the most widely used techniques for network segmentation is VLANs (Virtual Local Area Networks), which provide a logical separation of network traffic without the need for physical infrastructure changes. VLANs enable administrators to group devices logically, regardless of their physical location, into distinct broadcast domains, thereby controlling traffic flow and enforcing security policies more effectively. VLAN implementation typically involves configuring network switches to assign ports to specific VLANs based on defined criteria such as departmental affiliation, function, or security requirements. The process begins with VLAN creation, where administrators define the VLANs they need and assign each VLAN a unique VLAN ID. This ID serves as a tag that identifies and segregates traffic belonging to different VLANs as it traverses the network. To create a VLAN on a network switch, administrators can access the switch's command-line interface (CLI) and use the appropriate command, such as "vlan <vlan-id>", to define the VLAN and assign it a numerical identifier. Once VLANs are created, administrators must assign switch ports to the appropriate VLANs to control which devices are members of each VLAN. This process, known as VLAN membership configuration, involves specifying the VLAN membership mode for each switch port, either as an access port or a trunk port. An access port is typically assigned to a single VLAN and carries traffic only for that VLAN, while a trunk port can carry traffic for multiple VLANs simultaneously. Administrators can configure VLAN membership using commands such as "switchport mode access" or "switchport mode trunk" followed by additional parameters as needed. After assigning ports to VLANs, administrators may need to configure VLAN trunking to enable inter-VLAN communication and traffic routing between VLANs. Trunking allows switches to transport traffic for multiple VLANs over a single physical link, facilitating efficient use of network bandwidth and simplifying VLAN deployment. To configure trunking on a switch port, administrators can use commands like "switchport mode trunk" and "switchport trunk allowed vlan <vlan-list>", specifying the VLANs allowed to traverse the trunk link. In addition to VLAN creation and membership configuration, VLAN tagging is a critical aspect of VLAN implementation, especially in environments where VLAN traffic needs to traverse multiple network devices. VLAN tagging involves adding a VLAN tag, also known as a VLAN header, to Ethernet frames to indicate their VLAN membership. This tagging enables switches to differentiate between traffic from different VLANs and enforce VLAN-based policies accordingly. The most common VLAN tagging protocol is IEEE 802.1Q, which inserts a VLAN tag into the Ethernet frame header and specifies the VLAN ID associated with the frame. To configure VLAN tagging on a switch port, administrators can use commands like "switchport trunk encapsulation dot1q" to enable 802.1Q VLAN tagging on trunk ports. Once VLANs are configured and VLAN tagging is in place, administrators can implement VLAN-based security policies to control access to network resources and protect against unauthorized access and malicious activity. VLANs enable administrators to define access control lists (ACLs) and firewall rules based on VLAN membership, restricting traffic between VLANs and enforcing communication policies. For example, administrators can configure ACLs to allow or deny traffic between specific VLANs or between VLANs and external networks based on predefined criteria such as IP addresses, port numbers, or protocols. Additionally, VLANs can be used in conjunction with other security mechanisms such as VLAN access control lists (VACLs) and private VLANs (PVLANs) to further enhance network security and isolation. VACLs allow administrators to apply access control policies directly to VLAN traffic within the switch, while PVLANs enable finer-grained segmentation by dividing a single VLAN into multiple isolated sub-VLANs. Overall, VLANs are a powerful tool for implementing network segmentation and enhancing network security, performance, and manageability. By logically dividing the network into separate broadcast domains, VLANs enable administrators to isolate traffic, control access, and enforce security policies more effectively, thereby creating a more resilient and secure network infrastructure.

Chapter 7: Network Address Translation (NAT) and Port Forwarding

Network Address Translation (NAT) and port forwarding are fundamental concepts in modern networking, essential for enabling communication between devices in private networks and the internet. NAT allows multiple devices within a private network to share a single public IP address for outgoing internet connections, effectively masking the internal network topology from external networks. This process is crucial for conserving public IP addresses and enhancing network security by hiding internal IP addresses from potential attackers. In a typical NAT configuration, a NAT-enabled router or firewall translates the private IP addresses of devices within the local network into a single public IP address when communicating with external networks. This translation occurs transparently, with the router maintaining a NAT translation table to track the mapping between internal and external IP addresses and ports. To configure NAT on a router or firewall, administrators can access the device's configuration interface and use commands such as "ip nat inside" and "ip nat outside" to specify which interfaces are part of the internal (private) and external (public) networks, respectively. Additionally, administrators can configure NAT translation rules to define how traffic should be translated between the internal and external networks. These rules typically include criteria such as source and destination IP addresses, transport layer protocols (e.g., TCP, UDP), and port numbers. For example, a common NAT translation rule might specify that outgoing traffic from devices within the internal network should be translated to use the router's public IP address when communicating with external servers on the internet. NAT also plays a crucial role in facilitating communication between devices in different private networks by translating IP addresses and ports as necessary to route traffic between them. This capability is particularly useful in scenarios where organizations need to connect multiple branch offices or remote sites over the internet securely. In addition to NAT, port forwarding is another important networking technique used to direct incoming traffic from the internet to specific devices or services within a private network. Port forwarding allows administrators to expose services running on internal network devices, such as web servers, email servers, or gaming consoles, to the internet by forwarding incoming traffic destined for a specific port on the router to a corresponding port on an internal device. To configure port forwarding, administrators must define port forwarding rules on the router or firewall to specify which external ports should be forwarded to which internal IP addresses and ports. This configuration typically involves specifying the protocol (TCP or UDP), external port, internal IP address, and internal port for each forwarding rule. For example, to forward incoming HTTP (port 80) traffic to an internal web server with the IP address 192.168.1.100, administrators can use a command like "ip nat inside source static tcp 192.168.1.100 80 <public-ip> 80" to create the port forwarding rule on the router. Once configured, port forwarding allows external users to access the designated service on the internal device using the router's public IP address and the specified port number. Port forwarding is commonly used in scenarios where organizations host web servers, email servers, or other services internally and need to make them accessible from the internet while maintaining control over inbound traffic. However, it's essential to implement port forwarding carefully to avoid exposing sensitive services to potential security risks, such as unauthorized access or exploitation of vulnerabilities. Administrators should regularly review and update port forwarding rules to ensure they align with the organization's security policies and best practices. Additionally, they should consider implementing additional security measures, such as access control lists (ACLs) or intrusion detection/prevention systems (IDS/IPS), to monitor and protect against malicious activity targeting forwarded ports. In summary, NAT and port forwarding are essential networking techniques that enable organizations to efficiently manage and secure their network traffic, both internally and externally. By leveraging NAT, organizations can conserve public IP addresses, enhance network security, and enable communication between devices in private networks and the internet. Similarly, port forwarding allows organizations to expose internal services to the internet while maintaining control over inbound traffic, facilitating remote access and connectivity without compromising security. Configuring Network Address Translation (NAT) and port forwarding on routers is essential for managing and directing network traffic effectively. NAT allows routers to translate private IP addresses used within a local network into public IP addresses when communicating with external networks, conserving public IP address space and enhancing network security. To configure NAT on a router, administrators typically access the router's configuration interface, commonly through a web-based graphical user interface (GUI) or a command-line interface (CLI) via Telnet or SSH. Within the configuration interface, administrators can define NAT translation rules to specify how internal IP addresses should be translated to external IP addresses. For instance, on Cisco routers, administrators can use commands such as "ip nat inside" and "ip nat outside" to designate internal and external interfaces, respectively, and then create translation rules using the "ip nat inside source" command. These rules map internal IP addresses to external IP addresses and specify the type of translation (e.g., static NAT, dynamic NAT, or NAT overload). Static NAT maps specific internal IP addresses to specific external IP addresses, ensuring consistent one-to-one address translation for services like web servers or email servers. To configure static NAT, administrators use commands like "ip nat inside source static" followed by the internal and external IP addresses. Dynamic NAT, on the other hand, dynamically assigns external IP addresses from a pool of available addresses to internal devices as needed. Administrators define a pool of external IP addresses using the "ip nat pool" command and associate it with internal devices using the "ip nat inside source list" command along with an access control list (ACL) specifying the internal addresses. NAT overload, also known as Port Address Translation (PAT), allows multiple internal devices to share a single public IP address by translating their source port numbers along with their IP addresses. This technique is commonly used for internet access in home and small office networks. To configure NAT overload, administrators use the "ip nat inside source list" command with the "overload" keyword, along with an ACL specifying the internal addresses. Port forwarding, also referred to as port mapping or port redirection, is another crucial feature of routers that enables inbound traffic from the internet to be directed to specific devices or services within the local network. Port forwarding is commonly used to make services such as web servers, FTP servers, or gaming servers accessible from the internet. To configure port forwarding on a router, administrators create port forwarding rules that specify which external ports should be forwarded to which internal IP addresses and ports. For example, to forward incoming HTTP traffic on port 80 to an internal web server with IP address 192.168.1.100, administrators use commands like "ip nat inside source static tcp" followed by the internal IP address, internal port, and external port. Additionally, administrators may need to configure access control lists (ACLs) to permit inbound traffic on the specified ports and protocols. Once configured, NAT and port forwarding enable routers to efficiently manage network traffic, allowing internal devices to communicate with external networks and making internal services accessible from the internet. Administrators should regularly review and update NAT and port forwarding configurations to align with network requirements and security policies, ensuring optimal performance and protection against unauthorized access.

Chapter 8: Implementing VPNs for Secure Remote Access

Virtual Private Networks (VPNs) have become increasingly vital in today's interconnected digital landscape, providing secure and private communication channels over public networks such as the internet. A VPN extends a private network across a public network, enabling users to send and receive data as if their devices were directly connected to the private network. This technology is particularly valuable for remote workers, businesses, and individuals seeking to safeguard their online activities from prying eyes. VPNs employ various protocols and encryption techniques to ensure the confidentiality, integrity, and authenticity of transmitted data. One of the most commonly used VPN protocols is the Point-to-Point Tunneling Protocol (PPTP), which establishes a secure connection between the user's device and the VPN server. To initiate a PPTP VPN connection from the command line in Linux, users can utilize the "pptp" command followed by the VPN server's hostname or IP address. Another widely adopted VPN protocol is the Layer 2 Tunneling Protocol (L2TP), which combines the features of PPTP and the Layer 2 Forwarding (L2F) protocol. L2TP creates a tunnel between the user's device and the VPN server, encapsulating data packets for secure transmission. To configure an L2TP VPN connection in Linux, users typically use the "ipsec" command to manage IPsec security associations and policies and the "xl2tpd" command to handle L2TP tunneling. Additionally, the Internet Key Exchange (IKE) protocol is often used in conjunction with L2TP to establish secure communication channels and manage encryption keys. The OpenVPN protocol has gained popularity for its open-source nature and strong security features, including OpenSSL encryption and Transport Layer Security (TLS) authentication. OpenVPN creates a secure tunnel between the user's device and the VPN server, providing confidentiality and integrity for transmitted data. To deploy an OpenVPN server and client in Linux, users can install the "openvpn" package and configure server and client configuration files using a text editor such as "vi" or "nano." Once configured, users can initiate an OpenVPN connection using the "openvpn" command followed by the path to the client configuration file. Additionally, some VPN services offer proprietary protocols such as Cisco's AnyConnect or Juniper's Pulse Secure for enhanced security and compatibility with enterprise-grade VPN solutions. These protocols often require dedicated client software provided by the VPN service provider and are commonly used in corporate environments for remote access and secure communication. Beyond protocol selection, VPNs offer various deployment options to suit different needs and preferences. Site-to-Site VPNs, also known as router-to-router VPNs, connect multiple networks or remote offices securely over the internet, enabling seamless communication and resource sharing. To configure a Site-to-Site VPN, administrators typically configure VPN tunnels and routing policies on the participating routers or firewalls using vendor-specific configuration interfaces or command-line interfaces. Remote Access VPNs, on the other hand, allow individual users or devices to connect securely to a corporate network from remote locations. These VPNs are commonly used by telecommuters, mobile workers, and business travelers to access corporate resources such as email, files, and applications from anywhere with an internet connection. Remote Access VPNs can be implemented using dedicated VPN appliances, software-based VPN servers, or cloud-based VPN services, depending on the organization's requirements and infrastructure. Overall, VPNs play a crucial role in safeguarding data privacy, enhancing network security, and enabling secure remote access in today's interconnected world. Whether for personal privacy protection or corporate data security, understanding VPN technologies and deployment options is essential for individuals and organizations alike. Configuring Virtual Private Networks (VPNs) for both remote access and site-to-site connectivity is essential for organizations seeking to establish secure communication channels over public networks like the internet. Remote access VPNs enable individual users or devices to securely connect to a corporate network from remote locations, providing access to resources such as email, files, and applications. To configure a remote access VPN, organizations typically deploy VPN servers and client software capable of establishing encrypted tunnels between remote devices and the corporate network. One common approach is to utilize the OpenVPN protocol, known for its robust security features and cross-platform compatibility. To set up an OpenVPN server for remote access, administrators can install the "openvpn" package on a dedicated server or virtual machine and configure server settings and client profiles using configuration files and scripts. These configuration files specify parameters such as the VPN server's IP address, port number, encryption settings, and authentication methods. Once the server is configured, users can initiate VPN connections from their devices using OpenVPN client software and the provided configuration files. Alternatively, organizations may opt for proprietary VPN solutions such as Cisco AnyConnect or Pulse Secure for remote access VPN deployments. These solutions typically require the installation of dedicated client software provided by the VPN vendor, along with server-side configuration and management tools. In addition to remote access VPNs, organizations often deploy site-to-site VPNs to establish secure communication links between multiple networks or remote offices. Site-to-site VPNs, also known as router-to-router VPNs, enable seamless connectivity and resource sharing across geographically dispersed locations. To configure a site-to-site VPN, administrators typically configure VPN tunnels and routing policies on the participating routers or firewalls using vendor-specific configuration interfaces or command-line interfaces. For example, in a Cisco networking environment, administrators can use the Cisco Adaptive Security Appliance (ASA) or Cisco IOS routers to configure IPsec-based site-to-site VPNs using the "crypto" command-line interface (CLI) commands. These commands specify parameters such as the VPN tunnel endpoints, encryption algorithms, and pre-shared keys for secure communication. Once the VPN tunnels are established, traffic can flow securely between the connected networks, allowing users at different locations to access shared resources and services as if they were part of the same local network. Beyond IPsec-based VPNs, organizations may explore alternative technologies such as Multiprotocol Label Switching (MPLS) or software-defined WAN (SD-WAN) for site-to-site connectivity, depending on their specific requirements and infrastructure. MPLS-based VPNs offer reliable and predictable performance for mission-critical applications but may require significant upfront investment and ongoing maintenance. SD-WAN solutions, on the other hand, leverage software-defined networking (SDN) principles to dynamically route traffic across multiple network paths, optimizing performance and resilience. To deploy an SD-WAN solution for site-to-site connectivity, organizations typically deploy SD-WAN edge devices at each location and configure centralized policies and routing rules using a management console or controller. These policies dictate how traffic is prioritized, routed, and secured across the SD-WAN infrastructure, ensuring optimal performance and reliability for critical applications. Overall, configuring VPNs for remote access and site-to-site connectivity is a fundamental aspect of network security and connectivity for modern organizations. By implementing secure and reliable VPN solutions, organizations can facilitate remote work, enable seamless collaboration across distributed teams, and safeguard sensitive data from unauthorized access or interception.

Chapter 9: Intrusion Detection and Prevention Systems (IDS/IPS)

In modern cybersecurity, Intrusion Detection Systems (IDS) and Intrusion Prevention Systems (IPS) play a crucial role in safeguarding networks against various cyber threats and attacks. An IDS is a security tool designed to monitor network traffic or system activity for suspicious behavior or policy violations and alert administrators when such activity is detected. On the other hand, an IPS goes a step further by not only detecting but also actively blocking or preventing malicious activity in real-time. Deploying an IDS/IPS solution is essential for organizations seeking to enhance their security posture and protect critical assets from unauthorized access, data breaches, and other cyber threats. One popular open-source IDS/IPS solution is Snort, which offers robust traffic analysis capabilities and a vast library of pre-defined rules for detecting known threats and attack patterns. To deploy Snort, administrators can install the Snort package on a dedicated server or network appliance and configure it to monitor network traffic on specific interfaces or subnets. Using the Snort configuration file,

administrators can define rulesets to match against incoming and outgoing traffic and specify actions to take when suspicious activity is detected, such as generating alerts, logging events, or blocking traffic. For example, to enable Snort to monitor traffic on the eth0 interface, administrators can use the following command:
bash
Copy code
```
sudo snort -i eth0 -c /etc/snort/snort.conf
```
This command instructs Snort to listen on the eth0 interface and use the configuration file located at /etc/snort/snort.conf. Additionally, administrators can leverage Snort's rule management capabilities to create custom rules tailored to their organization's specific security requirements and threat landscape. These custom rules can be used to detect and alert on suspicious activity unique to the organization's environment, such as unauthorized access attempts, malware infections, or data exfiltration attempts. Beyond Snort, commercial IDS/IPS solutions such as Suricata and Cisco Firepower provide advanced threat detection and prevention capabilities, including support for protocol analysis, signature-based detection, and anomaly-based detection. These solutions offer centralized management consoles, real-time threat intelligence feeds, and

integration with other security tools for comprehensive threat management and incident response. When deploying an IDS/IPS solution, organizations should consider factors such as network topology, traffic volume, and regulatory compliance requirements to ensure effective coverage and protection against a wide range of cyber threats. Additionally, regular updates and maintenance are essential to keep the IDS/IPS solution up-to-date with the latest threat signatures and security patches, minimizing the risk of false positives and false negatives. Overall, IDS/IPS solutions are critical components of a layered security strategy, providing organizations with visibility into their network traffic and the ability to detect and respond to security incidents in real-time. By leveraging IDS/IPS technologies effectively, organizations can strengthen their defenses against evolving cyber threats and minimize the impact of security breaches on their operations and reputation.

Implementing and configuring Intrusion Detection Systems (IDS) and Intrusion Prevention Systems (IPS) is a crucial aspect of modern cybersecurity, essential for safeguarding networks against various cyber threats and attacks. IDS is a security solution designed to monitor network traffic or system activity for suspicious behavior or policy violations, while IPS takes it a step further by actively blocking or preventing malicious activity in real-time. Deploying an IDS/IPS solution involves several key steps, starting with selecting the appropriate software or hardware solution based on the organization's security requirements and budget constraints. One popular open-source IDS/IPS solution is Snort, renowned for its robust traffic analysis capabilities and extensive library of pre-defined rules for detecting known threats and attack patterns. To deploy Snort, administrators can install the Snort package on a dedicated server or network appliance and configure it to monitor network traffic on specific interfaces or subnets. This process typically involves editing the Snort configuration file to define rulesets, specify monitoring interfaces, and configure alerting and logging settings. For example, to enable Snort to monitor traffic on the eth0 interface, administrators can use the command:

bash

Copy code

```
sudo snort -i eth0 -c /etc/snort/snort.conf
```

This command instructs Snort to listen on the eth0 interface and use the configuration file located at /etc/snort/snort.conf. In addition to Snort, organizations may also consider commercial

IDS/IPS solutions such as Suricata and Cisco Firepower, which offer advanced threat detection and prevention capabilities, centralized management consoles, and real-time threat intelligence feeds. When deploying an IDS/IPS solution, it's essential to consider factors such as network topology, traffic volume, and regulatory compliance requirements to ensure effective coverage and protection against a wide range of cyber threats. Furthermore, regular updates and maintenance are critical to keeping the IDS/IPS solution up-to-date with the latest threat signatures and security patches, minimizing the risk of false positives and false negatives. Beyond deployment, configuring the IDS/IPS solution involves fine-tuning rule sets, thresholds, and alerting mechanisms to optimize detection accuracy and minimize the impact on network performance. Administrators should prioritize rules that align with the organization's specific security policies and threat landscape, customizing rule sets to detect and alert on suspicious activity relevant to their environment. Additionally, administrators should establish procedures for incident response and mitigation, defining workflows for investigating and responding to alerts generated by the IDS/IPS solution. This includes triaging alerts, analyzing network traffic logs, and taking appropriate actions to contain and remediate security incidents effectively. To ensure the ongoing effectiveness of the IDS/IPS solution, organizations should conduct regular security assessments and audits, evaluating the solution's performance against established security objectives and benchmarks. This may involve conducting penetration tests, vulnerability scans, and simulated cyber attack exercises to identify weaknesses and areas for improvement. By implementing and configuring IDS/IPS solutions effectively, organizations can strengthen their cybersecurity posture, detect and respond to security threats in a timely manner, and mitigate the risk of data breaches and network intrusions.

Chapter 10: Network Security Best Practices and Hardening Techniques

Securing network devices is paramount in maintaining the integrity and confidentiality of data transmitted across networks. With the proliferation of cyber threats targeting network infrastructure, implementing best practices for securing network devices has become increasingly critical. One fundamental aspect of securing network devices is ensuring that they are running the latest firmware or software updates. This includes patches for known vulnerabilities and security flaws that could be exploited by attackers. Most network devices provide CLI commands or web-based interfaces for updating firmware. For example, on Cisco devices, administrators can use the "show version" command to check the current firmware version and then download and install updates from the Cisco website. In addition to keeping firmware up-to-date, it's essential to change default passwords and disable unnecessary services to reduce the attack surface. Many network devices come with default login credentials, which are well-known and frequently targeted by attackers. By changing these default passwords to strong, unique passwords, administrators can significantly enhance the security posture of their network infrastructure. Furthermore, disabling unused services and protocols helps minimize the risk of exploitation and reduces the likelihood of unauthorized access. Network administrators can use CLI commands such as "no service telnet" or "no ip http server" on Cisco devices to disable Telnet and HTTP services, respectively. Another best practice for securing network devices is implementing access control lists (ACLs) to control traffic flow and restrict access to sensitive resources. ACLs allow administrators to define rules that permit or deny traffic based on various criteria, such as source IP address, destination IP address, protocol, and port number. For example, administrators can create an ACL to permit only specific IP addresses to access management interfaces or critical network services. On Cisco routers and switches, ACLs are configured using the "access-list" command, followed by rules specifying the permitted or denied traffic. Additionally, network segmentation is a fundamental security principle that helps contain and isolate potential security breaches. By dividing the network into separate segments or VLANs based on functional requirements or security policies, organizations can limit the impact of a compromised device or unauthorized access. VLANs can be configured on network switches using CLI commands such as "vlan" and "interface vlan," assigning specific ports to each VLAN and implementing inter-VLAN routing as needed. Regularly monitoring network traffic and logging events is essential for detecting and responding to security incidents promptly. Network devices typically support logging capabilities that allow administrators to capture and analyze network activity for signs of malicious behavior or unauthorized access attempts. By enabling logging and configuring syslog servers to receive log messages, administrators can centralize log management and perform in-depth analysis of network events. Cisco devices support syslog logging with commands such as "logging host" to specify the IP address of the syslog server and "logging trap" to set the severity level of log messages. Additionally, implementing encryption protocols such as SSH (Secure Shell) and HTTPS (Hypertext Transfer Protocol Secure) for remote management helps protect sensitive data transmitted between network devices and management consoles. SSH provides secure, encrypted access to network devices' CLI interfaces, while HTTPS encrypts web-based management traffic. Administrators can enable SSH and HTTPS on network devices using CLI commands such as "ip ssh version 2" and "ip http secure-server" on Cisco devices. Finally, conducting regular security audits and assessments is crucial for identifying vulnerabilities and weaknesses in network infrastructure. Penetration testing, vulnerability scanning, and configuration audits can help organizations proactively identify and address security gaps before they can be exploited by attackers. By following these best practices and adopting a proactive approach to network security, organizations can mitigate the risk of cyber threats and safeguard their critical assets and data.

Hardening network infrastructure against common attacks is essential for safeguarding critical assets and ensuring the integrity, confidentiality, and availability of data. One of the most fundamental steps in network hardening is implementing strong access controls to restrict unauthorized access to network resources. Access controls can be enforced through the use of access control lists (ACLs), which allow administrators to define rules that permit or deny traffic based on various criteria, such as source and destination IP addresses, ports, and protocols.

For example, on Cisco devices, administrators can use the "access-list" command to create ACLs and apply them to interfaces using the "ip access-group" command. Additionally, disabling unnecessary services and protocols helps reduce the attack surface and minimize the risk of exploitation. Many network devices come with default services and protocols enabled, which may not be required for normal operation. By disabling these unnecessary services, administrators can mitigate potential security risks. CLI commands such as "no service telnet" and "no ip http server" can be used on Cisco devices to disable Telnet and HTTP services, respectively. Furthermore, enforcing strong authentication mechanisms, such as multifactor authentication (MFA) and certificate-based authentication, helps prevent unauthorized access to network devices. MFA requires users to provide multiple forms of verification, such as a password and a one-time code sent to their mobile device, before granting access. Certificate-based authentication relies on digital certificates issued to trusted users and devices, ensuring that only authorized entities can access the network. On Cisco devices, administrators can configure MFA using the "aaa authentication" command and certificate-based authentication using the "crypto pki" command.

Regularly updating and patching network devices is crucial for addressing known vulnerabilities and security flaws that could be exploited by attackers. Vendors frequently release updates and patches to fix security vulnerabilities identified in their products. Administrators should regularly check for updates and apply them as soon as possible to maintain the security of their network infrastructure. CLI commands such as "show version" can be used to check the current firmware version on Cisco devices, and updates can be downloaded and installed from the vendor's website. Implementing intrusion detection and prevention systems (IDS/IPS) helps detect and block malicious activity on the network. IDS/IPS solutions monitor network traffic for signs of suspicious behavior or known attack patterns and take action to prevent unauthorized access or malicious activity. Cisco devices support IDS/IPS functionality through features such as Cisco Intrusion Prevention System (IPS) and Cisco Adaptive Security Appliance (ASA). Administrators can configure these features using CLI commands such as "ips" and "threat-detection." Additionally, encrypting sensitive data in transit and at rest helps protect it from unauthorized access and interception by attackers. Encryption protocols such as SSL/TLS for data in transit and encryption algorithms such as AES for data at rest provide strong cryptographic protection against eavesdropping and data theft. On Cisco devices, administrators can enable SSL/TLS encryption for network communications using the "ssl encryption" command and encrypt sensitive data stored on devices using encryption algorithms supported by the device's operating system. Conducting regular security audits and assessments is essential for identifying and addressing security vulnerabilities in network infrastructure. Penetration testing, vulnerability scanning, and security assessments help organizations identify weaknesses and gaps in their security posture and take remedial actions to mitigate them. By following these best practices and adopting a proactive approach to network hardening, organizations can significantly enhance the security of their network infrastructure and protect against common cyber threats.

BOOK 4

RHCSA EXAM PASS

PERFORMANCE TUNING AND TROUBLESHOOTING TECHNIQUES

ROB BOTWRIGHT

Chapter 1: Understanding System Performance Metrics and Monitoring Tools

Introduction to system performance metrics is crucial for understanding and optimizing the performance of computer systems and networks. System performance metrics provide valuable insights into the health, efficiency, and utilization of hardware resources such as CPU, memory, disk, and network interfaces. By monitoring these metrics, administrators can identify performance bottlenecks, troubleshoot issues, and optimize system configurations to improve overall performance. One of the most fundamental system performance metrics is CPU utilization, which measures the percentage of time the CPU spends executing instructions. High CPU utilization can indicate resource contention and may lead to degraded system performance. Administrators can monitor CPU utilization using commands like "top" on Unix-based systems or "Task Manager" on Windows systems. Memory utilization is another critical performance metric that measures the amount of physical memory used by the system. High memory utilization can result in paging or swapping, where the system moves data between RAM and disk, causing performance degradation. Commands like "free" on Unix-based systems or "Resource Monitor" on Windows systems can be used to monitor memory utilization. Disk I/O (input/output) performance metrics measure the speed at which data is read from and written to disk storage. High disk I/O can indicate storage bottlenecks and may lead to slow application response times. Commands like "iostat" on Unix-based systems or "Performance Monitor" on Windows systems can provide insights into disk I/O performance. Network utilization metrics track the amount of data transmitted and received over network interfaces. High network utilization can indicate network congestion or bandwidth limitations, affecting the performance of networked applications. Commands like "ifconfig" or "netstat" on Unix-based systems or "Resource Monitor" on Windows systems can be used to monitor network utilization. In addition to these primary performance metrics, there are numerous other metrics that administrators may monitor depending on their specific needs and environment. These may include metrics related to process activity, disk space utilization, system uptime, and more. Collecting and analyzing system performance metrics over time allows administrators to establish performance baselines, detect trends, and proactively address potential issues before they impact users. Various monitoring tools and utilities are available to automate the collection and analysis of system performance metrics. These tools range from simple command-line utilities to sophisticated monitoring platforms with graphical interfaces and advanced analytics capabilities. Some popular open-source monitoring tools include Nagios, Zabbix, and Prometheus, while commercial offerings include SolarWinds, Datadog, and New Relic. Regardless of the tools used, effective monitoring and analysis of system performance metrics require careful planning, configuration, and ongoing maintenance. Administrators must select appropriate metrics to monitor based on their environment and performance objectives, configure monitoring tools to collect and store metric data, set up alerting thresholds to notify administrators of potential issues, and regularly review and analyze metric data to identify trends and patterns. By mastering the fundamentals of system performance metrics and employing effective monitoring and analysis techniques, administrators can optimize the performance, reliability, and availability of their computer systems and networks, ensuring a positive user experience and minimizing downtime and disruptions.

An overview of system monitoring tools is essential for administrators tasked with maintaining the health, performance, and security of computer systems and networks. System monitoring tools provide real-time insights into various aspects of system operation, enabling administrators to detect issues, troubleshoot problems, and optimize system performance. One of the most widely used system monitoring tools is Nagios, an open-source monitoring solution that allows administrators to monitor the availability and performance of network services, host resources, and environmental factors. Nagios uses plugins to collect data from different systems and applications, providing a centralized dashboard for monitoring and alerting. Another popular system monitoring tool is Zabbix, which offers a comprehensive platform for monitoring the performance and availability of IT infrastructure components. Zabbix supports a wide range of monitoring protocols and can monitor various metrics, including CPU, memory, disk, and network usage. Administrators can configure triggers and notifications to alert them of potential issues in real-time. Prometheus is another notable system monitoring tool widely used in modern cloud-native environments. Developed as an open-source project, Prometheus is designed for monitoring highly dynamic and distributed systems. It uses a pull-based model to collect metrics from targets such as application servers, databases, and containers. Prometheus stores collected metrics in a time-series database and provides a powerful query language for analysis and visualization. Grafana is often used in conjunction with Prometheus to create customizable dashboards and visualizations of system metrics. Grafana supports integration with various data sources, including Prometheus, allowing administrators to create rich, interactive dashboards to monitor system performance. In addition to these open-source tools, there are numerous commercial system monitoring solutions available in the market, offering advanced features and support options. SolarWinds Orion is a comprehensive network monitoring platform that provides real-time visibility into network performance, health, and availability. Orion offers features such as network device discovery, performance monitoring, and alerting, making it a popular choice for enterprise environments. Datadog is another commercial system monitoring solution that offers a unified monitoring platform for cloud-scale applications and infrastructure. Datadog supports monitoring of cloud services, containers, microservices, and more, providing insights into system performance, logs, and traces. Splunk is a widely used platform for monitoring and analyzing machine-generated data, including logs, events, and metrics. Splunk ingests data from various sources and provides powerful search and analytics capabilities for troubleshooting, security analysis, and business intelligence. Microsoft System Center Operations Manager (SCOM) is a comprehensive monitoring solution for Microsoft environments, providing end-to-end monitoring of applications, servers, and network devices. SCOM offers features such as performance monitoring, alerting, and reporting, helping administrators ensure the health and availability of their Microsoft infrastructure. In summary, system monitoring tools play a crucial role in maintaining the performance, availability, and security of computer systems and networks. Whether open-source or commercial, these tools provide administrators with the visibility and insights needed to effectively monitor, manage, and optimize their IT infrastructure. By leveraging the capabilities of system monitoring tools, administrators can proactively identify issues, mitigate risks, and ensure the reliability and performance of their systems and services.

Chapter 2: Analyzing System Resource Usage and Bottlenecks

Identifying resource bottlenecks is a critical aspect of system administration, essential for maintaining optimal performance and stability within an IT infrastructure. Resource bottlenecks occur when a particular resource, such as CPU, memory, disk I/O, or network bandwidth, becomes saturated and limits the overall performance of the system. Detecting and resolving these bottlenecks requires a systematic approach that involves monitoring system metrics, analyzing performance data, and identifying potential sources of contention. One of the most common tools used to identify resource bottlenecks is the top command, which provides a real-time view of system processes and resource usage. By running the top command in the terminal, administrators can quickly identify processes that are consuming excessive CPU or memory resources, helping them pinpoint potential bottlenecks. Additionally, the vmstat command can be used to monitor system-wide resource usage, including CPU, memory, disk, and network activity. By analyzing the output of vmstat, administrators can identify patterns of resource usage and potential bottlenecks that may be impacting system performance. Another useful tool for identifying resource bottlenecks is the iostat command, which provides information about disk I/O activity and performance. By running iostat with appropriate options, administrators can identify disks that are experiencing high levels of I/O activity or latency, indicating potential bottlenecks in disk performance. Similarly, the sar command can be used to collect and analyze system activity data over time, providing insights into resource usage patterns and potential bottlenecks. By regularly collecting and analyzing data with sar, administrators can identify trends and patterns that may indicate underlying performance issues. In addition to command-line tools, administrators can also use graphical monitoring tools such as Grafana and Prometheus to visualize system metrics and identify resource bottlenecks. These tools provide customizable dashboards and visualizations that allow administrators to monitor system performance in real-time and detect anomalies or bottlenecks. When investigating resource bottlenecks, it's essential to consider the specific characteristics of the workload and the underlying hardware infrastructure. For example,

CPU-bound workloads may indicate a need for additional processing power or optimization of software algorithms, while memory-bound workloads may require additional RAM or tuning of memory management settings. Similarly, disk I/O-bound workloads may benefit from faster storage devices or optimization of disk access patterns. Network bottlenecks can often be alleviated by upgrading network hardware, optimizing network configurations, or implementing network traffic shaping and prioritization techniques. Once a resource bottleneck has been identified, administrators can take steps to address the issue and optimize system performance. This may involve upgrading hardware components, tuning system configurations, optimizing software applications, or redistributing workloads across multiple systems. By regularly monitoring system performance and proactively addressing resource bottlenecks, administrators can ensure the smooth operation of their IT infrastructure and minimize the impact of performance issues on end-users and applications. In summary, identifying resource bottlenecks is a critical task for system administrators, requiring the use of monitoring tools, analysis techniques, and diagnostic strategies to pinpoint performance issues and optimize system performance. By leveraging command-line tools, graphical monitoring solutions, and best practices for performance analysis, administrators can effectively identify and resolve resource bottlenecks, ensuring the reliability, scalability, and responsiveness of their IT infrastructure.

Using monitoring tools to analyze resource usage is a fundamental aspect of system administration, allowing administrators to gain insights into the performance and health of their IT infrastructure. These tools provide valuable data on various system resources such as CPU, memory, disk I/O, and network bandwidth, enabling administrators to identify bottlenecks, troubleshoot issues, and optimize system performance. One commonly used monitoring tool is Nagios, an open-source platform that offers comprehensive monitoring capabilities for network services, host resources, and environmental factors. By deploying Nagios and configuring it to monitor critical components of the infrastructure, administrators can receive alerts and notifications about potential issues before they escalate into problems. Another popular monitoring tool is Zabbix, which provides real-time monitoring, alerting, and visualization features for IT infrastructure components. With Zabbix, administrators can monitor performance metrics, track trends over time, and generate reports to analyze resource usage patterns and identify potential issues. In addition to these open-source solutions, many organizations use commercial monitoring tools such as SolarWinds, Datadog, and New Relic, which offer advanced features and support for a wide range of technologies. These tools provide comprehensive monitoring capabilities, including real-time performance monitoring, log analysis, and application performance management (APM), helping administrators gain deep insights into the health and performance of their infrastructure. When analyzing resource usage with monitoring tools, administrators typically focus on key metrics such as CPU utilization, memory usage, disk I/O rates, and network traffic. By monitoring these metrics over time and setting thresholds for acceptable performance levels, administrators can proactively identify issues and take corrective action before they impact users or applications. For example, administrators may use the top command to monitor CPU usage and identify processes that are consuming excessive CPU resources. By analyzing the output of top and identifying CPU-intensive processes, administrators can prioritize resource allocation and optimize system performance. Similarly, administrators may use tools such as sar and vmstat to monitor memory usage and identify potential memory leaks or excessive memory consumption by processes. By analyzing memory usage patterns and identifying processes that are consuming large amounts of memory, administrators can take steps to optimize memory usage and prevent performance degradation. Disk I/O monitoring is another critical aspect of resource usage analysis, as disk I/O bottlenecks can significantly impact system performance. Administrators may use tools such as iostat and sar to monitor disk I/O rates, latency, and throughput, helping them identify disks that are experiencing high levels of I/O activity or performance issues. By analyzing disk I/O metrics and identifying potential bottlenecks, administrators can optimize disk configurations, redistribute workloads, or upgrade storage hardware to improve performance. Network monitoring is also essential for analyzing resource usage and identifying potential issues such as network congestion, packet loss, or latency. Administrators may use tools such as iftop, netstat, and nload to monitor network traffic and identify bandwidth-intensive applications or devices. By analyzing network traffic patterns and identifying potential bottlenecks, administrators can optimize network configurations, implement Quality of Service (QoS) policies, or upgrade network hardware to improve performance and reliability. In addition to monitoring system resources, administrators may also use log analysis tools such as ELK Stack (Elasticsearch, Logstash, Kibana) or Splunk to analyze log data and identify potential issues or security threats. These tools allow administrators to centralize log data from various sources, analyze log entries in real-time, and create alerts and dashboards to monitor system activity and detect anomalies. By analyzing log data and identifying potential issues or security incidents, administrators can proactively address issues and mitigate risks to the infrastructure. In summary, using monitoring tools to analyze resource usage is essential for maintaining the performance, reliability, and security of IT infrastructure. By monitoring key metrics such as CPU, memory, disk I/O, and network traffic, administrators can identify bottlenecks, troubleshoot issues, and optimize system performance. Whether using open-source or commercial monitoring solutions, administrators can leverage these tools to gain deep insights into resource usage patterns, detect anomalies, and ensure the smooth operation of their infrastructure.

Chapter 3: Performance Tuning Techniques for CPU and Memory Optimization

CPU performance tuning is a crucial aspect of optimizing system performance, ensuring efficient resource utilization, and enhancing overall productivity in computing environments. To begin optimizing CPU performance, administrators often start with analyzing the current CPU usage and identifying any potential bottlenecks or areas for improvement. This can be achieved by using various monitoring tools such as top, htop, or sar, which provide real-time insights into CPU usage, process activity, and system performance metrics. By running these commands and observing CPU utilization levels, administrators can gain an understanding of how CPU resources are being utilized and identify any processes or applications that are consuming excessive CPU cycles. Once potential bottlenecks are identified, administrators can employ various tuning strategies to optimize CPU performance and improve system responsiveness. One common tuning strategy is process prioritization, where administrators use the nice and renice commands to adjust the priority of CPU-bound processes. By assigning higher priorities to critical processes and lower priorities to less important tasks, administrators can ensure that essential applications receive the necessary CPU resources while preventing non-critical processes from monopolizing CPU time. Additionally, administrators may utilize CPU affinity settings to bind specific processes or threads to particular CPU cores. This can be achieved using the taskset command, which allows administrators to specify CPU affinity masks and control which CPU cores are used by individual processes. By assigning processes to dedicated CPU cores, administrators can minimize CPU contention and improve overall system performance, particularly in multi-core systems. Another effective CPU tuning strategy is to optimize system and kernel parameters to better align with workload requirements and hardware capabilities. This involves adjusting various kernel parameters such as scheduler settings, interrupt handling, and CPU scaling governors to optimize CPU performance for specific workloads. For example, administrators may adjust the CPU scheduler to prioritize interactive tasks over background processes or configure CPU scaling governors to dynamically adjust CPU frequencies based on workload demands. By fine-tuning these parameters, administrators can optimize CPU performance and achieve better responsiveness and efficiency in handling various workloads. Additionally, administrators may explore hardware-level optimizations to further enhance CPU performance. This may involve upgrading CPU hardware to newer models with higher clock speeds, more cores, or improved architectures to better meet the demands of modern applications and workloads. Alternatively, administrators may consider overclocking CPUs within safe operating limits to achieve higher performance levels, although this approach requires careful consideration of potential risks and trade-offs. Moreover, optimizing CPU performance also involves monitoring and managing system thermal conditions to prevent overheating and maintain stable operation. Administrators can use tools like lm_sensors or htop to monitor CPU temperatures and fan speeds and take appropriate measures to mitigate overheating risks, such as improving system ventilation, adjusting fan speeds, or installing additional cooling solutions. By ensuring optimal thermal management, administrators can prevent CPU throttling and maintain consistent performance levels under varying workload conditions. Furthermore, administrators may consider workload optimization techniques to distribute CPU-intensive tasks more evenly across systems and reduce contention for CPU resources. This may involve load balancing techniques such as task distribution, workload partitioning, or parallel processing to distribute CPU-intensive tasks across multiple systems or CPU cores efficiently. Additionally, administrators can optimize application code and algorithms to minimize CPU overhead and improve overall performance. By optimizing CPU performance through a combination of tuning strategies, hardware upgrades, workload optimizations, and thermal management techniques, administrators can achieve significant improvements in system responsiveness, efficiency, and reliability. These efforts not only enhance user experience and productivity but also ensure that computing resources are utilized optimally to meet the demands of modern workloads and applications.

Memory optimization is a critical aspect of enhancing system performance and ensuring efficient resource utilization in computing environments. One fundamental memory optimization technique is to analyze memory usage and identify any potential inefficiencies or areas for improvement. This can be achieved by using monitoring tools such as free, top, or vmstat, which provide real-time insights into memory utilization, swap usage, and system performance metrics. By running these commands and observing memory usage patterns, administrators can gain an understanding of how memory resources are being utilized and identify any processes or applications that are consuming excessive memory. Once potential inefficiencies are identified, administrators can employ various memory optimization strategies to improve system performance and responsiveness. One common optimization technique is to identify and optimize memory-intensive processes or applications. Administrators can use tools like top or htop to identify processes that are consuming significant amounts of memory and investigate their resource usage patterns. By analyzing these processes, administrators can determine if they are memory-bound and take appropriate actions to optimize their memory usage. This may involve tuning application configurations, optimizing database queries, or reducing memory footprint through code optimization techniques.

Additionally, administrators can utilize memory management tools such as malloc_trim or madvise to release unused memory back to the system, improving overall memory utilization and reducing memory fragmentation. Another memory optimization technique is to adjust system-level memory parameters to better align with workload requirements and hardware capabilities. This involves tuning various kernel parameters such as swappiness, page cache settings, or memory allocation policies to optimize memory usage for specific workloads. For example, administrators may adjust the swappiness parameter to control the balance between swapping and caching, ensuring that memory resources are used efficiently based on workload demands. Additionally, administrators may adjust page cache settings to prioritize file system caching or optimize memory allocation policies to improve memory utilization and reduce memory fragmentation. Moreover, administrators can employ memory compression techniques to reduce memory usage and improve system responsiveness. Memory compression algorithms such as zswap or zram compress memory pages in real-time, allowing more data to be stored in memory and reducing the need for swapping to disk. By compressing memory pages, administrators can effectively increase the amount of available memory and improve system performance, particularly on systems with limited physical memory. Additionally, administrators can utilize memory deduplication techniques to identify and eliminate duplicate memory pages, further reducing memory usage and improving overall system efficiency. Memory deduplication tools such as KSM (Kernel Samepage Merging) or deduplication-enabled file systems can identify identical memory pages and consolidate them into a single shared page, saving memory resources and reducing memory overhead.

Furthermore, administrators may consider upgrading memory hardware to increase system capacity and improve performance. This may involve adding more RAM modules, upgrading to faster memory types, or installing memory with higher capacity to better meet the demands of modern workloads and applications. Additionally, administrators can employ memory mirroring or RAID configurations to enhance memory reliability and fault tolerance, ensuring data integrity and system stability in the event of memory failures. By optimizing memory performance through a combination of tuning strategies, memory management techniques, hardware upgrades, and fault tolerance measures, administrators can achieve significant improvements in system responsiveness, efficiency, and reliability. These efforts not only enhance user experience and productivity but also ensure that memory resources are utilized optimally to meet the demands of modern computing environments.

Chapter 4: Optimizing Disk I/O Performance and Storage Configuration

Disk I/O performance optimization is a crucial aspect of system tuning and is essential for ensuring efficient data access and storage operations in computing environments. One fundamental strategy for optimizing disk I/O performance is to analyze disk usage patterns and identify potential bottlenecks or areas for improvement. This can be achieved using various monitoring tools such as iostat, sar, or atop, which provide insights into disk I/O activity, throughput, and latency. By running these commands and analyzing their output, administrators can gain an understanding of how disks are being utilized and identify any processes or applications that are generating excessive disk I/O activity. Once potential bottlenecks are identified, administrators can implement various optimization strategies to improve disk I/O performance. One common optimization technique is to optimize file system configurations to better align with workload requirements and hardware capabilities. This involves selecting the appropriate file system type and tuning various file system parameters to optimize disk I/O performance. For example, administrators can choose between different file system types such as ext4, XFS, or Btrfs, depending on their specific requirements for performance, reliability, and features. Additionally, administrators can adjust file system parameters such as block size, journaling mode, or inode size to optimize disk I/O performance for specific workloads. Another optimization strategy is to use disk partitioning and layout techniques to improve disk I/O performance. By partitioning disks into separate partitions or volumes and placing data and system files strategically, administrators can minimize disk contention and optimize data access patterns. For example, administrators can create separate partitions for system files, application data, and log files to isolate I/O operations and prevent them from interfering with each other. Additionally, administrators can use RAID (Redundant Array of Independent Disks) configurations to improve disk I/O performance and reliability. RAID configurations such as RAID 0 (striping) or RAID 10 (mirroring and striping) can distribute data across multiple disks and improve read and write performance by parallelizing I/O operations. Moreover, administrators can employ disk caching techniques to reduce disk I/O latency and improve overall system responsiveness. Disk caching mechanisms such as read-ahead caching, write-back caching, or disk-based caching solutions can cache frequently accessed data in memory or on disk, reducing the need for disk I/O operations and improving application performance. By caching data in memory or on disk, administrators can reduce disk I/O latency and improve application responsiveness, particularly for read-heavy workloads. Additionally, administrators can optimize disk I/O performance by using solid-state drives (SSDs) or flash storage devices. SSDs offer significantly faster read and write speeds compared to traditional hard disk drives (HDDs) and can dramatically improve disk I/O performance for both random and sequential I/O operations. By replacing HDDs with SSDs or using hybrid storage solutions that combine HDDs and SSDs, administrators can achieve substantial improvements in disk I/O performance and overall system responsiveness. Furthermore, administrators can implement disk I/O scheduling algorithms to optimize disk I/O performance and prioritize critical I/O operations. Disk I/O scheduling algorithms such as CFQ (Completely Fair Queuing), deadline, or noop can adjust the order in which I/O requests are processed and optimize disk I/O performance based on workload characteristics and system requirements. By selecting the appropriate disk I/O scheduling algorithm and tuning its parameters, administrators can improve disk I/O performance and ensure that critical I/O operations are processed in a timely manner. Additionally, administrators can monitor disk I/O performance metrics regularly using monitoring tools such as iostat or atop and adjust optimization strategies as needed to adapt to changing workload conditions or system requirements. By continuously monitoring disk I/O performance and optimizing disk I/O operations, administrators can ensure efficient data access and storage operations, improve system responsiveness, and enhance overall system performance.

Storage configuration best practices are essential guidelines for effectively managing storage resources in a computing environment, ensuring optimal performance, reliability, and scalability. One fundamental best practice is to leverage redundant storage configurations, such as RAID (Redundant Array of Independent Disks), to improve data availability and protect against hardware failures. RAID configurations, including RAID 1 (mirroring), RAID 5 (striping with parity), and RAID 10 (striping and mirroring), distribute data across multiple disks and provide fault tolerance by storing redundant copies of data or parity information. By implementing RAID configurations, organizations can minimize the risk of data loss due to disk failures and ensure continuous access to critical data. Another best practice is to use storage tiering to optimize performance and cost-efficiency. Storage tiering involves categorizing data into different tiers based on its access frequency, importance, and performance requirements, and storing each tier on storage media with appropriate performance characteristics and costs. For example, organizations can use high-performance solid-state drives (SSDs) for storing frequently accessed and performance-sensitive data, while using lower-cost hard disk drives (HDDs) for storing less frequently accessed or archival data. By tiering storage resources, organizations can optimize storage performance and costs, ensuring that critical data is stored on high-performance storage media while minimizing expenses for less frequently accessed data. Additionally, organizations should implement data deduplication and compression techniques to optimize storage utilization and reduce storage costs. Data deduplication removes duplicate copies of data within a storage system, eliminating redundant data and reclaiming storage space. Compression techniques reduce the size of data by encoding it using algorithms that remove redundant information and store it in a more compact form. By deduplicating and compressing data, organizations can maximize storage efficiency, reduce storage footprint, and lower storage costs. Another key best practice is to implement data replication and backup strategies to protect against data loss and ensure data availability. Data replication involves creating duplicate copies of data and storing them on separate storage systems or geographical locations to provide redundancy and protect against hardware failures, disasters, or data corruption. Backup strategies involve regularly backing up data to secondary storage systems or backup media and storing copies off-site to protect against data loss due to hardware failures, disasters, or human errors. By implementing data replication and backup strategies, organizations can ensure data availability, minimize downtime, and recover from data loss events quickly and effectively. Additionally, organizations should regularly monitor and optimize storage performance to identify bottlenecks, resource constraints, or capacity issues proactively.

Monitoring tools such as iostat, sar, or atop provide insights into storage performance metrics such as I/O throughput, latency, and utilization, allowing administrators to identify performance issues and optimize storage configurations accordingly. By monitoring storage performance regularly and tuning storage configurations as needed, organizations can ensure optimal storage performance, reliability, and scalability. Furthermore, organizations should consider scalability and future growth when designing storage configurations, ensuring that storage systems can accommodate increasing data volumes and evolving workload requirements over time. Scalable storage architectures such as scale-out storage clusters or cloud-based storage solutions provide flexibility and agility to scale storage resources horizontally or vertically to meet changing demands. By designing storage configurations with scalability in mind, organizations can future-proof their storage infrastructure and avoid costly and disruptive storage upgrades in the future. Overall, storage configuration best practices encompass a range of strategies and techniques for effectively managing storage resources, optimizing performance, ensuring data availability, and minimizing costs. By following these best practices, organizations can maximize the value of their storage investments, improve operational efficiency, and mitigate risks associated with data storage and management.

Chapter 5: Network Performance Tuning and Optimization Strategies

Network performance metrics and analysis play a crucial role in assessing and optimizing the efficiency, reliability, and responsiveness of computer networks. These metrics provide valuable insights into network behavior, traffic patterns, and resource utilization, enabling network administrators to identify performance bottlenecks, troubleshoot issues, and improve overall network performance. One essential network performance metric is bandwidth, which measures the maximum data transfer rate between two points in a network and is typically expressed in bits per second (bps). Bandwidth represents the capacity of the network link and influences the speed at which data can be transmitted. To measure bandwidth, network administrators can use tools such as iperf or speedtest-cli to perform bandwidth tests between network endpoints and assess the available bandwidth. Another critical network performance metric is latency, which measures the time it takes for a data packet to travel from its source to its destination and back. Latency is a key determinant of network responsiveness and application performance, particularly for real-time applications such as voice and video conferencing. Network administrators can use tools such as ping or traceroute to measure latency and identify network delays or packet loss issues. Packet loss is another important network performance metric that measures the percentage of data packets lost during transmission over a network link. Packet loss can occur due to network congestion, hardware failures, or network configuration issues and can impact application performance and user experience. Network administrators can use tools such as ping or traceroute with packet loss monitoring options to detect packet loss and troubleshoot its underlying causes. Throughput is another essential network performance metric that measures the rate at which data is successfully transmitted between network endpoints and is typically expressed in bits per second (bps) or packets per second (pps). Throughput reflects the actual data transfer rate achieved on a network link and is influenced by factors such as bandwidth, latency, and packet loss. Network administrators can use tools such as iperf or netperf to measure throughput and assess the efficiency of network communication. Jitter is a network performance metric that measures the variation in packet arrival times at a destination and is a key factor in determining the quality of real-time multimedia applications such as voice and video streaming. High jitter can result in packet reordering, delay, and poor application performance. Network administrators can use tools such as ping or jitter test utilities to measure jitter and assess network stability and reliability. Quality of Service (QoS) is a network performance metric that measures the ability of a network to deliver traffic with different priority levels according to predefined service level agreements (SLAs). QoS mechanisms such as traffic shaping, prioritization, and queuing ensure that critical traffic types such as voice and video are given preferential treatment over less critical traffic types such as email or web browsing. Network administrators can use tools such as tc (traffic control) or QoS management platforms to configure and monitor QoS policies and ensure that network resources are allocated efficiently. Network performance analysis involves collecting, analyzing, and interpreting network performance metrics to identify performance issues, trends, and optimization opportunities. Network administrators can use tools such as Wireshark, Nagios, or Zabbix to capture network traffic, monitor network devices, and generate performance reports. By analyzing network performance metrics over time, administrators can detect anomalies, predict future performance trends, and implement proactive measures to improve network performance and reliability. Overall, network performance metrics and analysis are essential components of effective network management, enabling organizations to optimize network resources, maximize performance, and deliver a superior user experience. Through continuous monitoring, analysis, and optimization, organizations can ensure that their networks meet the demands of modern business applications and support the evolving needs of their users.

Network optimization techniques are essential strategies employed to enhance the performance, efficiency, and reliability of computer networks. These techniques aim to maximize the utilization of network resources while minimizing latency, packet loss, and other factors that may degrade network performance. One common network optimization technique is traffic prioritization, which involves assigning different priority levels to network traffic based on its importance or criticality. This ensures that mission-critical applications such as voice and video conferencing receive preferential treatment over less time-sensitive traffic like email or web browsing. Administrators can implement traffic prioritization using Quality of Service (QoS) mechanisms such as DiffServ (Differentiated Services) or MPLS (Multiprotocol Label Switching). Another network optimization technique is bandwidth management, which involves controlling and allocating available bandwidth to ensure equitable distribution among users and applications. Bandwidth management techniques include traffic shaping, bandwidth throttling, and link aggregation, which help prevent network congestion and ensure optimal performance for all network users. Administrators can configure bandwidth management policies using tools like tc (traffic control) or network appliances like routers and switches. Network caching is another effective optimization technique that involves storing frequently accessed data locally to reduce the need for repeated requests to remote servers. By caching web pages, files, and multimedia content at strategic points in the network, such as proxy servers or content delivery networks (CDNs), organizations can accelerate content delivery, improve response times, and reduce bandwidth consumption. Popular caching solutions include Squid for web caching and

Varnish for HTTP reverse proxy caching. Protocol optimization is another important technique for improving network performance, particularly in environments with high-latency or unreliable connections. Protocol optimization involves optimizing the behavior of network protocols to reduce overhead, minimize round-trip times, and improve overall efficiency. Techniques such as TCP window scaling, selective acknowledgments (SACK), and protocol-specific optimizations for applications like HTTP and FTP can significantly enhance network performance in challenging environments. Network compression is another effective optimization technique that involves reducing the size of data packets transmitted over the network to minimize bandwidth usage and improve transmission speeds. Compression techniques such as gzip, deflate, and LZMA can be applied to various types of network traffic, including web content, email attachments, and file transfers, to reduce data volume without sacrificing quality. Network redundancy and failover mechanisms are critical optimization techniques for ensuring high availability and reliability in network infrastructure. Redundancy techniques such as link aggregation, redundant links, and network clustering help eliminate single points of failure and ensure continuous operation in the event of hardware failures or network disruptions. Failover mechanisms such as Virtual Router Redundancy Protocol (VRRP) and Hot Standby Router Protocol (HSRP) automatically redirect traffic to backup links or devices in the event of a primary link or device failure, minimizing downtime and ensuring uninterrupted service. Network optimization also encompasses techniques for improving wireless network performance, such as optimizing coverage, reducing interference, and enhancing roaming capabilities. Techniques such as site surveys, channel planning, and antenna placement optimization help optimize Wi-Fi networks for maximum coverage, capacity, and performance. Advanced features like beamforming, MU-MIMO (Multi-User Multiple Input Multiple Output), and band steering can further enhance wireless network performance in high-density environments. In summary, network optimization techniques are essential for maximizing the performance, efficiency, and reliability of computer networks. By implementing traffic prioritization, bandwidth management, caching, protocol optimization, compression, redundancy, and other optimization techniques, organizations can ensure optimal network performance and deliver a superior user experience. Through continuous monitoring, analysis, and optimization, network administrators can identify areas for improvement, implement best practices, and optimize network infrastructure to meet the evolving needs of their users and applications.

Chapter 6: Tuning Kernel Parameters for Enhanced System Performance

Understanding kernel parameters is crucial for optimizing the performance, stability, and functionality of a Linux system. Kernel parameters, also known as sysctl settings, are configuration options that control various aspects of the Linux kernel's behavior. These parameters are stored in the /proc/sys directory and can be modified at runtime using the sysctl command or by editing configuration files in /etc/sysctl.d. One common use case for kernel parameters is tuning network performance. By adjusting parameters related to network buffer sizes, TCP congestion control algorithms, and other network-related settings, administrators can optimize network throughput, reduce latency, and improve overall network performance. For example, the net.core.rmem_max and net.core.wmem_max parameters control the maximum receive and transmit socket buffer sizes, respectively. Increasing these values can help prevent packet loss and improve network performance, especially on high-speed networks with large round-trip times. Similarly, the net.ipv4.tcp_congestion_control parameter allows administrators to specify the TCP congestion control algorithm used by the kernel. Popular congestion control algorithms include Cubic, BBR, and Reno, each with its own characteristics and performance trade-offs. By experimenting with different algorithms and tuning parameters like initial congestion window size and slow start threshold, administrators can optimize TCP/IP throughput and responsiveness for specific network conditions and workloads. Kernel parameters are also used to adjust memory management settings to optimize system performance and resource utilization. Parameters like vm.swappiness control the tendency of the kernel to swap out memory pages to disk under memory pressure. By adjusting swappiness and other memory-related parameters, administrators can fine-tune the balance between using physical memory and swap space, which can impact system responsiveness and overall performance.

Disk I/O performance can also be optimized using kernel parameters related to the I/O scheduler, disk elevator algorithm, and filesystem cache settings. For example, the vm.dirty_background_ratio and vm.dirty_ratio parameters control the percentage of system memory used for buffering dirty (modified) data before it is written to disk. By adjusting these parameters, administrators can balance disk I/O performance and system responsiveness based on workload characteristics and available system resources. Security is another important aspect of kernel parameter tuning. Parameters like kernel.randomize_va_space control Address Space Layout Randomization (ASLR), which helps prevent certain types of security vulnerabilities, such as buffer overflow attacks. Additionally, parameters like kernel.sysrq allow administrators to enable or disable specific kernel features, such as the ability to trigger a kernel panic or perform low-level debugging tasks via the Magic SysRq key combination. It's important for administrators to carefully review and understand the implications of each kernel parameter before making changes, as incorrect settings can potentially degrade system performance, stability, or security.

Documentation for kernel parameters can typically be found in the kernel source tree, kernel documentation, or online resources such as the Linux Kernel Parameters website. Additionally, many Linux distributions provide default values and recommended settings for kernel parameters in their documentation or support forums. In summary, understanding kernel parameters is essential for optimizing the performance, stability, and security of a Linux system. By adjusting parameters related to networking, memory management, disk I/O, and security, administrators can tailor the system configuration to meet the specific requirements of their workloads and applications. Continuous monitoring, experimentation, and documentation are key practices for effectively managing kernel parameters and maintaining optimal system performance over time.

Configuring kernel parameters for performance tuning is a fundamental aspect of optimizing the behavior and efficiency of a Linux system. These parameters, also known as sysctl settings, allow administrators to fine-tune various aspects of the Linux kernel's operation to better suit specific workloads and hardware configurations. Understanding how to identify, modify, and apply appropriate kernel parameters is essential for achieving optimal system performance and responsiveness. One of the primary tools for managing kernel parameters is the sysctl command, which provides a convenient interface for viewing, modifying, and persisting changes to sysctl settings. For example, the sysctl -a command can be used to display the current values of all kernel parameters, while sysctl <parameter_name> allows administrators to view or modify the value of a specific parameter. Kernel parameters are typically stored in the /proc/sys directory and organized into a hierarchical structure that reflects different subsystems and settings. This directory contains a series of files corresponding to individual parameters, which can be read from or written to like regular text files. To modify a kernel parameter permanently, administrators can add entries to configuration files in the /etc/sysctl.d directory or modify the /etc/sysctl.conf file directly. Each entry in these configuration files specifies a kernel parameter name followed by its desired value, separated by an equals sign. For example, to set the value of the vm.swappiness parameter to 10, administrators can add a line like vm.swappiness=10 to the sysctl.conf file. Once changes have been made to the sysctl configuration files, administrators can apply them by running the sysctl -p command, which reloads the configuration and applies the new parameter values. When it comes to performance tuning, kernel parameters can be adjusted to optimize various aspects of system behavior, including CPU scheduling, memory management, disk I/O, and networking. For example, parameters related to CPU scheduling and process management, such as kernel.sched_min_granularity_ns and kernel.sched_wakeup_granularity_ns, control the scheduling granularity and wakeup behavior of the kernel's process scheduler. By adjusting these parameters, administrators can fine-tune CPU scheduling to better balance system responsiveness and throughput under different workload conditions. Memory management parameters, such as vm.dirty_ratio and vm.dirty_background_ratio, control the behavior of the kernel's disk writeback mechanism, which determines when dirty (modified) memory pages are flushed to disk. By adjusting these parameters, administrators can optimize the balance between memory usage and disk I/O performance based on available system resources and workload characteristics. Disk I/O performance can be further optimized by adjusting parameters related to the kernel's I/O scheduler, elevator algorithm, and filesystem cache settings. For example, parameters like vm.vfs_cache_pressure and vm.dirty_writeback_centisecs control the behavior of the kernel's filesystem cache, which caches frequently accessed disk blocks and directory entries to improve read and write performance. Networking parameters, such as net.core.rmem_max and net.core.wmem_max, control the maximum size of receive and transmit socket buffers, respectively. By adjusting these parameters, administrators can optimize network throughput and latency for specific network conditions and workloads. It's important for administrators to carefully review and understand the implications of each kernel parameter before making changes, as incorrect settings can potentially degrade system performance or stability. Documentation for kernel parameters can typically be found in the kernel source tree, kernel documentation, or online resources such as the Linux Kernel Parameters website. Additionally, many Linux distributions provide default values and recommended settings for kernel parameters in their documentation or support forums.

Continuous monitoring, experimentation, and documentation are key practices for effectively managing kernel parameters and maintaining optimal system performance over time. In summary, configuring kernel parameters for performance tuning is a critical aspect of optimizing the behavior and efficiency of a Linux system. By understanding how to identify, modify, and apply appropriate kernel parameters, administrators can fine-tune various aspects of system behavior to better suit specific workloads and hardware configurations, ultimately improving system performance, responsiveness, and efficiency.

Chapter 7: Troubleshooting Common Performance Issues and Errors

Identifying and resolving performance issues in a computing environment is a crucial task for system administrators and IT professionals. Performance issues can manifest in various ways, including slow response times, high resource utilization, and application errors. To effectively address these issues, it's essential to follow a systematic approach that involves monitoring, analysis, troubleshooting, and optimization. One of the first steps in identifying performance issues is to establish baseline metrics for system performance. This involves collecting data on key performance indicators such as CPU usage, memory utilization, disk I/O, and network throughput over a period of time. Tools like sar, top, vmstat, and iostat can be used to gather this data and identify patterns or anomalies that may indicate performance problems. Once baseline metrics have been established, administrators can monitor system performance regularly to detect deviations from normal behavior. This proactive approach allows them to identify potential issues before they impact end users or critical business processes. When performance issues arise, the next step is to conduct thorough analysis to identify the root cause. This typically involves examining system logs, error messages, and performance metrics to pinpoint the source of the problem. For example, if a system is experiencing high CPU utilization, administrators may use tools like ps, top, or htop to identify the processes consuming the most CPU resources. Similarly, if disk I/O is a bottleneck, tools like iostat or blktrace can be used to analyze disk activity and identify processes or applications generating high I/O load. Network performance issues can be analyzed using tools like iftop, netstat, or tcpdump to monitor network traffic and identify potential bottlenecks or connectivity problems. Once the root cause of a performance issue has been identified, administrators can take steps to resolve the problem and optimize system performance. This may involve making configuration changes, applying patches or updates, optimizing application code, or adding hardware resources to address resource constraints. For example, if a database server is experiencing slow query performance, administrators may optimize database indexes, adjust query parameters, or add additional memory or CPU resources to improve performance. Similarly, if a web server is experiencing high latency, administrators may optimize web server configuration settings, compress content, or implement caching mechanisms to reduce load times. In some cases, performance issues may require more advanced troubleshooting techniques, such as kernel tuning, network optimization, or application profiling. This may involve using tools like strace, perf, or tcpdump to trace system calls, analyze performance bottlenecks, or debug network traffic. Additionally, collaboration with application developers, database administrators, or network engineers may be necessary to identify and resolve complex performance issues that span multiple layers of the technology stack. Continuous monitoring and optimization are key practices for maintaining optimal system performance over time. This involves regularly reviewing performance metrics, identifying areas for improvement, and implementing changes to address evolving workload requirements. Additionally, periodic performance testing and capacity planning can help identify potential performance bottlenecks and ensure that systems are adequately provisioned to handle expected workloads. By following a systematic approach to identifying and resolving performance issues, administrators can ensure that systems operate efficiently and reliably to meet the needs of users and applications. Troubleshooting performance errors is a critical task for system administrators and IT professionals, requiring a systematic approach to identify and resolve issues efficiently. Performance errors can manifest in various forms, including slow response times, application crashes, and system freezes, impacting user productivity and disrupting business operations. To effectively troubleshoot performance errors, it's essential to gather relevant information and analyze system behavior to identify the root cause. One common approach is to start by examining system logs, which can provide valuable insights into the events leading up to the error. Commands like "tail", "grep", and "journalctl" can be used to search for error messages and exceptions in log files, helping administrators pinpoint the source of the problem. Additionally, monitoring tools like "top", "htop", and "sar" can provide real-time information on system resource usage, helping identify potential bottlenecks or abnormal behavior. When troubleshooting performance errors, it's essential to consider both hardware and software factors that may contribute to the problem. Hardware issues such as insufficient memory, disk failures, or network connectivity problems can all impact system performance and should be investigated thoroughly. Commands like "free", "df", and "ifconfig" can be used to gather information about system hardware and network interfaces, helping administrators identify potential hardware-related issues. In addition to hardware problems, software issues such as misconfigured applications, buggy code, or outdated software versions can also cause performance errors. Administrators may need to use debugging tools like "strace" or "gdb" to trace application execution and identify potential software bugs. Furthermore, updating software packages, applying patches, or reinstalling problematic applications may be necessary to resolve software-related performance errors. Network-related issues can also contribute to performance errors, especially in environments with complex network configurations or high network traffic. Commands like "netstat", "tcpdump", and "traceroute" can be used to diagnose network connectivity issues, packet loss, or latency problems, helping administrators troubleshoot network-related performance errors. Additionally, examining network switch and router configurations, analyzing firewall rules, and monitoring network traffic patterns can help identify and resolve performance issues related to network infrastructure. In some cases, performance errors may be caused by external factors such as denial-of-service (DoS) attacks, malware infections, or hardware failures beyond the administrator's control. In these situations, administrators may need to work with security teams, vendors, or third-party experts to mitigate the impact of external threats and restore normal system operation. Moreover, implementing proactive measures such as regular system maintenance, security updates, and disaster recovery planning can help minimize the risk of performance errors and mitigate their impact on business operations. Collaborating with other stakeholders, including end users, application developers, and business analysts, is also crucial for effectively troubleshooting performance errors. By sharing information, coordinating efforts, and leveraging collective expertise, organizations can expedite the resolution of performance issues and minimize downtime. Additionally, documenting troubleshooting procedures, maintaining detailed records of performance incidents, and conducting post-mortem analyses can help organizations learn from past experiences and improve their ability to troubleshoot performance errors in the future. In summary, troubleshooting performance errors requires a systematic and collaborative approach that involves gathering relevant information, analyzing system behavior, and addressing both hardware and software factors that may contribute to the problem. By following best practices and leveraging appropriate tools and techniques, administrators can effectively identify and resolve performance errors to ensure the reliability and performance of IT systems.

Chapter 8: Analyzing System Logs for Performance Insights

Understanding performance-related log entries is essential for diagnosing and troubleshooting issues that affect the performance of computer systems. Log entries provide valuable insights into the behavior of software applications, hardware components, and the overall system environment. By analyzing performance-related log entries, administrators can identify anomalies, track resource utilization, and pinpoint the root causes of performance degradation. One common type of performance-related log entry is the error message, which indicates that an unexpected condition or problem has occurred within the system. Error messages often contain valuable information about the nature of the issue, including error codes, timestamps, and descriptions of the problem. For example, an error message in the Apache web server log might indicate that a client request failed due to insufficient server resources or a misconfiguration in the web server software. Another type of performance-related log entry is the warning message, which alerts administrators to potential issues or abnormal conditions that may impact system performance. Warning messages often serve as early indicators of problems that could escalate into more serious issues if left unaddressed. For instance, a warning message in the system log might indicate that disk space is running low, prompting administrators to take proactive measures to free up space and prevent system downtime. In addition to error and warning messages, performance-related log entries may also include informational messages that provide details about system events, processes, and resource usage. Informational messages can help administrators monitor system activity, track changes, and identify patterns that may affect performance. For example, an informational message in the syslog might indicate that a scheduled task has been successfully completed, providing confirmation that a system maintenance operation has been executed as expected. Analyzing performance-related log entries often involves using command-line tools such as "grep", "awk", and "sed" to search, filter, and extract relevant information from log files. For example, administrators can use the "grep" command to search for specific keywords or patterns within log files, allowing them to quickly locate performance-related entries. Similarly, the "awk" command can be used to extract specific fields or columns from log entries, facilitating further analysis and troubleshooting. Moreover, the "sed" command can be employed to perform text manipulation tasks such as substituting text, deleting lines, or filtering log entries based on specified criteria. By leveraging these command-line tools, administrators can efficiently parse through large volumes of log data and extract meaningful insights to diagnose and resolve performance issues. It's important for administrators to understand the context in which performance-related log entries occur and to correlate them with other system metrics and events. For example, administrators may need to examine CPU, memory, and disk utilization metrics alongside log entries to identify performance bottlenecks and resource constraints. Furthermore, administrators should pay attention to the frequency and recurrence of performance-related log entries to determine whether they represent isolated incidents or ongoing issues that require immediate attention. In summary, understanding performance-related log entries is crucial for maintaining the reliability, availability, and performance of computer systems. By analyzing error, warning, and informational messages in log files and correlating them with other system metrics, administrators can effectively diagnose and troubleshoot performance issues, enabling them to optimize system performance and minimize downtime. Analyzing system logs for performance insights is a fundamental aspect of maintaining the health and stability of computer systems, as logs serve as a rich source of information regarding the activities, events, and errors that occur within a system's environment. System logs contain valuable data that can offer deep insights into the performance of various components such as hardware, software, and network services. By effectively analyzing these logs, administrators can identify potential issues, diagnose problems, and optimize system performance. One of the most common types of system logs is the syslog, which records messages from the operating system kernel, system daemons, and user-level applications. The syslog typically resides in the "/var/log" directory on Unix-like systems and contains a variety of log files, each serving a specific purpose. For example, the "messages" log file captures general system messages, while the "auth.log" file records authentication-related events. Analyzing these logs involves examining the entries chronologically, looking for patterns or anomalies that may indicate performance issues or errors. Administrators can use commands like "grep," "tail," and "awk" to filter, search, and extract relevant information from log files. For instance, the "grep" command can be employed to search for specific keywords or phrases within log files, allowing administrators to focus on entries related to performance metrics or errors. Additionally, the "tail" command enables administrators to view the most recent entries in a log file, providing real-time insights into system activity. Meanwhile, the "awk" command can be used to extract specific fields or columns from log entries, facilitating further analysis and troubleshooting. Another critical aspect of analyzing system logs for performance insights is understanding the context in which events occur. Administrators must correlate log entries with other system metrics such as CPU usage, memory utilization, and disk I/O to gain a comprehensive understanding of system performance. For example, a sudden spike in CPU usage observed in performance monitoring tools may coincide with entries in the syslog indicating high levels of system activity or resource contention. By correlating these events, administrators can identify the root cause of performance issues and take appropriate actions to address them.

Moreover, it's essential to establish baseline performance metrics and monitor deviations from these baselines over time. Baseline metrics provide a point of reference for assessing system performance and detecting abnormal behavior. Administrators can use tools like "sar," "vmstat," and "top" to collect and analyze performance metrics regularly. These tools provide valuable insights into CPU, memory, disk, and network usage, allowing administrators to detect trends and anomalies that may impact system performance. Additionally, administrators should configure log rotation and retention policies to ensure that log files do not consume excessive disk space or become unwieldy to manage. Log rotation tools like "logrotate" automate the process of compressing and archiving old log files, making it easier to manage and analyze historical data. By implementing effective log management practices, administrators can maintain a clean and organized log directory while preserving valuable historical data for analysis and troubleshooting purposes. In summary, analyzing system logs for performance insights is a critical task for system administrators tasked with maintaining the health and stability of computer systems. By leveraging commands like "grep," "tail," and "awk" to search, filter, and extract relevant information from log files, administrators can gain valuable insights into system behavior and identify potential performance issues. Moreover, correlating log entries with other system metrics and establishing baseline performance metrics are essential practices for effectively monitoring and optimizing system performance. By adopting these practices, administrators can proactively identify and address performance issues, ensuring the reliability and availability of critical IT infrastructure.

Chapter 9: Implementing Profiling and Benchmarking Tools

Introduction to profiling and benchmarking is crucial for understanding the performance characteristics of software applications and systems, providing valuable insights into their behavior under various conditions. Profiling involves analyzing the execution of a program to identify bottlenecks, hotspots, and inefficiencies in code execution. By examining factors such as CPU usage, memory consumption, and I/O operations, developers and system administrators can pinpoint areas for optimization and improvement. One common tool for profiling is "perf," a powerful command-line tool for analyzing performance-related events on Linux systems. With "perf," users can gather detailed information about CPU utilization, cache misses, context switches, and more, helping to identify performance bottlenecks and areas for optimization. Another popular profiling tool is "gprof," which generates call graphs and execution profiles for C and C++ programs, enabling developers to visualize the flow of execution and identify functions that consume the most CPU time. Additionally, "strace" is a useful tool for profiling system calls, allowing users to monitor the interactions between a program and the operating system, including file I/O, network communication, and process management. Benchmarking, on the other hand, involves measuring the performance of a system or application against a known set of standards or criteria. By running standardized tests and comparing results, benchmarking enables users to assess the relative performance of different hardware configurations, software versions, or optimization techniques. One widely used benchmarking tool is "sysbench," which provides a flexible framework for running a variety of performance tests, including CPU, memory, file I/O, and database benchmarks. With "sysbench," users can simulate real-world workloads and measure the performance of their systems under different scenarios, helping to identify hardware limitations and performance bottlenecks. Another popular benchmarking tool is "iperf," which measures network bandwidth and latency by generating and transmitting TCP or UDP traffic between two hosts. By conducting network performance tests with "iperf," users can evaluate the throughput and latency of their network connections, identifying potential bottlenecks and optimizing network configurations for maximum performance. Furthermore, "bonnie++" is a tool commonly used for benchmarking disk I/O performance, providing insights into the read and write speeds of storage devices, as well as the impact of filesystem and RAID configurations on performance. By running "bonnie++" tests on different storage setups, users can evaluate the performance of their storage subsystems and make informed decisions about hardware upgrades or tuning parameters. In summary, profiling and benchmarking are essential techniques for understanding and optimizing the performance of software applications and systems. By leveraging tools like "perf," "gprof," "strace," "sysbench," "iperf," and "bonnie++," users can gain valuable insights into CPU, memory, disk, and network performance, helping to identify bottlenecks, optimize resource utilization, and improve overall system efficiency. Whether developing software applications, deploying infrastructure, or managing IT environments, profiling and benchmarking provide valuable tools for performance analysis and optimization, enabling users to achieve optimal performance and scalability. Using tools for performance profiling and benchmarking is essential for optimizing software applications and systems, providing valuable insights into their behavior and performance characteristics. One commonly used tool for performance profiling is "perf," which allows users to gather detailed information about CPU utilization, memory usage, and other system-level metrics. With "perf," users can analyze the performance of their applications and identify areas for optimization by examining factors such as cache misses, context switches, and CPU instructions retired. Another powerful tool for performance profiling is "gprof," which generates execution profiles and call graphs for C and C++ programs, enabling developers to visualize the flow of execution and identify functions that consume the most CPU time. By analyzing the output of "gprof," users can pinpoint performance bottlenecks and prioritize optimization efforts accordingly. Additionally, "strace" is a useful tool for profiling system calls, allowing users to monitor the interactions between a program and the operating system. With "strace," users can trace system calls, signals, and process events, providing insights into file I/O, network communication, and other system-level activities. In the realm of benchmarking, "sysbench" is a versatile tool for running performance tests on various system components, including CPU, memory, file I/O, and database performance. With "sysbench," users can simulate real-world workloads and measure the performance of their systems under different scenarios, helping to identify hardware limitations and performance bottlenecks. Another popular benchmarking tool is "iperf," which measures network bandwidth and latency by generating and transmitting TCP or UDP traffic between two hosts. By conducting network performance tests with "iperf," users can evaluate the throughput and latency of their network connections, identifying potential bottlenecks and optimizing network configurations for maximum performance. Furthermore, "bonnie++" is a tool commonly used for benchmarking disk I/O performance, providing insights into the read and write speeds of storage devices, as well as the impact of filesystem and RAID configurations on performance. By running "bonnie++" tests on different storage setups, users can evaluate the performance of their storage subsystems and make informed decisions about hardware upgrades or tuning parameters. In summary, using tools for performance profiling and benchmarking is essential for optimizing software applications and systems. By leveraging tools like "perf," "gprof," "strace," "sysbench," "iperf," and "bonnie++," users can gain valuable insights into CPU, memory, disk, and network performance, helping to identify bottlenecks, optimize resource utilization, and improve overall system efficiency. Whether developing software applications, deploying infrastructure, or managing IT environments, performance profiling and benchmarking provide valuable tools for performance analysis and optimization, enabling users to achieve optimal performance and scalability.

Chapter 10: Advanced Troubleshooting Techniques and Case Studies

Advanced performance troubleshooting techniques are essential for identifying and resolving complex performance issues that may arise in software applications or systems. These techniques go beyond basic monitoring and profiling to delve deeper into the root causes of performance degradation and inefficiency. One such technique is kernel-level tracing using tools like "strace" and "perf_events," which allow users to trace system calls, interrupts, and other kernel events to pinpoint performance bottlenecks at the operating system level. By analyzing the output of these tools, users can identify problematic system calls, excessive context switches, and other kernel-related issues that may impact overall system performance. Another advanced technique is user-level tracing using tools like "ptrace" and "SystemTap," which enable users to trace the execution of specific processes or threads within an application. With "ptrace," users can monitor system calls, signals, and memory accesses for individual processes, providing detailed insights into their behavior and performance characteristics. Similarly, "SystemTap" allows users to create custom tracing scripts to capture and analyze events at the user level, helping to diagnose performance issues related to application code, libraries, or system interactions. Additionally, advanced performance troubleshooting often involves analyzing performance counters and hardware events using tools like "perf" and "pmcstat." These tools allow users to monitor CPU performance metrics such as cache misses, branch mispredictions, and instruction-level events to identify performance bottlenecks at the hardware level. By correlating hardware performance data with software metrics, users can gain a comprehensive understanding of system behavior and optimize performance accordingly. Moreover, advanced performance troubleshooting may involve analyzing system-wide performance metrics using tools like "sar" and "vmstat," which provide detailed insights into CPU, memory, disk, and network utilization over time. By monitoring these metrics, users can identify trends and patterns that may indicate performance issues or resource contention, allowing them to take proactive measures to optimize system performance. Furthermore, advanced performance troubleshooting techniques often include analyzing application-level metrics using profiling tools like "gprof" and "Valgrind." These tools enable users to profile the execution of their applications, identify hotspots in the code, and optimize performance-critical sections for maximum efficiency. By analyzing the call graph, memory usage, and CPU time of their applications, users can optimize algorithms, data structures, and code paths to improve overall performance. Additionally, advanced performance troubleshooting may involve using performance modeling and simulation tools to predict the impact of proposed changes on system performance. By simulating different scenarios and workload patterns, users can evaluate the performance implications of configuration changes, code optimizations, or hardware upgrades before implementing them in production. This proactive approach helps to minimize the risk of performance regressions and ensures that system changes are aligned with performance goals. In summary, advanced performance troubleshooting techniques are essential for identifying and resolving complex performance issues in software applications and systems. By leveraging kernel-level tracing, user-level tracing, hardware performance monitoring, system-wide metrics analysis, application profiling, and performance modeling, users can gain deep insights into system behavior and optimize performance for maximum efficiency and scalability. Whether diagnosing CPU bottlenecks, memory leaks, disk I/O issues, or network latency problems, advanced performance troubleshooting techniques provide valuable tools and methodologies for optimizing system performance and ensuring a smooth user experience.

Case studies of complex performance issues and solutions provide valuable insights into real-world scenarios where performance problems have been identified and resolved. These case studies illustrate the challenges faced by organizations and the strategies they employed to overcome them. One such case study involves a web application experiencing slow response times during peak traffic hours. Upon investigation, it was discovered that the database server was overwhelmed by the sheer volume of queries being executed simultaneously. To address this issue, the organization implemented database query optimization techniques, such as indexing frequently accessed columns and rewriting inefficient queries. Additionally, they scaled up the database server by adding more CPU cores

and RAM to handle the increased workload. As a result of these optimizations, the web application's response times improved significantly, and users experienced faster page load times even during peak traffic periods.
Another case study revolves around a distributed system experiencing intermittent connectivity issues between its nodes. Upon analysis, it was found that network latency and packet loss were occurring due to suboptimal network configurations and hardware failures. To resolve these issues, the organization implemented network optimization techniques, such as configuring Quality of Service (QoS) policies to prioritize traffic, replacing faulty network switches and cables, and tuning TCP/IP parameters to minimize retransmissions. Additionally, they deployed network monitoring tools like "ping" and "traceroute" to identify network bottlenecks and troubleshoot connectivity issues in real-time. By addressing these underlying network issues, the organization was able to improve the reliability and performance of its distributed system, ensuring seamless communication between its nodes.

In another scenario, a high-traffic e-commerce website experienced frequent downtime and slow page load times, leading to a loss in revenue and customer dissatisfaction. Upon investigation, it was discovered that the website's infrastructure was not adequately scaled to handle the influx of traffic during peak shopping seasons. To address this issue, the organization implemented auto-scaling policies using cloud infrastructure providers like Amazon Web Services (AWS) or Google Cloud Platform (GCP). These auto-scaling policies dynamically provisioned additional compute resources, such as virtual machines or containers, based on predefined thresholds for CPU utilization, memory usage, and network traffic. Additionally, they optimized the website's frontend and backend code to reduce page load times and minimize server-side processing overhead. As a result of these optimizations, the e-commerce website's performance improved significantly, and downtime occurrences were drastically reduced, leading to higher customer satisfaction and increased revenue.

Furthermore, a software development company encountered performance issues with its flagship application, which was experiencing frequent crashes and memory leaks. Upon analysis, it was discovered that the application's codebase contained inefficient algorithms, resource-intensive processes, and memory leaks caused by improper memory management. To address these issues, the development team conducted a comprehensive code review and refactoring process, optimizing critical code paths, reducing memory usage, and implementing garbage collection strategies to reclaim unused memory. Additionally, they utilized memory profiling tools like "Valgrind" and "Heaptrack" to identify memory leaks and performance bottlenecks in the application's code. By addressing these underlying issues and optimizing the application's resource utilization, the development team was able to stabilize the application, improve its performance, and deliver a more reliable user experience to its customers.

In summary, case studies of complex performance issues and solutions provide valuable lessons for organizations seeking to optimize the performance of their software applications and systems. By analyzing real-world scenarios and the strategies employed to address them, organizations can gain insights into common performance problems, best practices for troubleshooting and optimization, and the tools and techniques available to improve system performance. Whether addressing database performance issues, network connectivity issues, scalability challenges, or software performance bottlenecks, case studies offer practical examples of how organizations can overcome complex performance issues and ensure the reliability, availability, and responsiveness of their systems.

Conclusion

In summary, the "RHCSA Exam Pass" book bundle offers a comprehensive and structured approach to preparing for the Red Hat Certified System Administrator (RHCSA) exam. With its four carefully curated books covering the foundational principles of Linux administration, advanced system configuration and management, network administration and security, and performance tuning and troubleshooting techniques, this bundle equips aspiring system administrators with the knowledge and skills necessary to succeed in the certification journey.

Book 1, "RHCSA Exam Pass: Foundations of Linux Administration," lays the groundwork by covering essential concepts such as file system navigation, user and group management, permissions, and basic shell scripting. It provides a solid foundation upon which learners can build their understanding of Linux systems and operations.

Book 2, "RHCSA Exam Pass: Advanced System Configuration and Management," delves deeper into system configuration topics, including service management with systemd, disk partitioning, file system optimization, and repository configuration. Readers will gain proficiency in managing complex system configurations and optimizing system resources for improved performance.

Book 3, "RHCSA Exam Pass: Network Administration and Security," explores network configuration, DNS, DHCP, firewalls, VPNs, and security measures. By mastering these topics, candidates will be able to design, configure, and secure network infrastructures in a Red Hat environment, ensuring the integrity and confidentiality of data transmission.

Book 4, "RHCSA Exam Pass: Performance Tuning and Troubleshooting Techniques," equips learners with the skills needed to optimize system performance and troubleshoot common issues. From analyzing system logs and monitoring performance metrics to identifying and resolving performance bottlenecks, this book provides invaluable insights into maintaining system health and efficiency.

Collectively, these four books offer a comprehensive and structured approach to preparing for the RHCSA exam, covering all essential topics and providing hands-on exercises and real-world scenarios to reinforce learning. Whether you are a novice seeking to enter the field of Linux system administration or an experienced professional aiming to validate your skills with certification, the "RHCSA Exam Pass" book bundle is your ultimate guide to success.

www.ingramcontent.com/pod-product-compliance
Lightning Source LLC
Chambersburg PA
CBHW071236050326
40690CB00011B/2140